Praise for *Protecting Innocence*

"Because of Detective Diane ~~...~~ with Crimes Against Children, she is an expert and her insights show on every page. Although I've read dozens of books on the topic, *Protecting Innocence* is the most practical and easy-to-read book I've seen on protecting our children."

— **Cecil Murphey**
New York Times best selling author
Childhood sexual abuse survivor

"Detective Diane Obbema's book, *Protecting Innocence*, boldly cuts through the veil of fear and embarrassment that surrounds the topic of child sexual abuse. This book offers clear and practical advice to parents on how they can keep their children safe from predators, and what they should do in the event that sexual abuse is disclosed. *Protecting Innocence* is a must-read for anyone in a position to protect children or affect change on their behalf. I whole-heartedly recommend this book to my patients."

— **Robin Eskey, PsyD**
Licensed Clinical Psychologist
Denver, Colorado

"Detective Obbema has dedicated the majority of her professional career investigating crimes against the most vulnerable and innocent individuals in our society. Her book, *Protecting Innocence*, contains real life examples and experiences that parents and others can learn from. I highly recommend this book to parents, teachers and other professionals."

— **Sheriff Ted Mink**
Jefferson County Sheriff's Office
Golden, Colorado

"In *Protecting Innocence*, Detective Obbema has written a very practical book on how parents and concerned adults can help protect children from sexual abuse. Her many years in this field interviewing parents, children, and perpetrators has given her insight into what to look for and how to talk with children at an age appropriate level to help them recognize and express discomfort with relationships that are heading into abuse. Every parent should read Protecting Innocence."

— **David Martin, MSW (Ret.)**
Foster Placement Team Supervisor
Department of Children and Family Services
Chicago, Illinois

"*Protecting Innocence* is an amazing book! It is compelling reading. I didn't want to put it down."

— **Dana Jene Easter, J.D.**
Chief Deputy District Attorney
Crimes Against Children
First Judicial District - Colorado

"Detective Obbema writes in an engaging style and clearly lays out everything you need to know about the mechanics of promoting the sexual safety of your child. Parents and childcare professionals will learn critical skills on how to relate and appropriately communicate with children. If five stars is tops, I give *Protecting Innocence* a ten!"

— **Phil P. Baca, Chief of Police (Ret.)**

Commerce City, Colorado

"It is easy to parent out of fear instead of confident love. In *Protecting Innocence*, your words have empowered my parenting skills, and helped me to clearly know what makes a child vulnerable. Thank you for this book!"

— **Mother of three**

Ages 4, 7, 12

Protecting Innocence

How to Discuss
Sexual Safety with Children

Detective Diane Obbema
Crimes Against Children Unit

Foreword by
Kathryn Wells MD, FAAP

Diane Obbema

HIGHDALE PRESS

Published by

HIGHDALE PRESS

Website: www.ProtectingInnocence.com
Email: DetectiveDiane@gmail.com

Editor and Illustrator: Rick Marschall
Cover and Interior Design: Nick Zelinger, NZ Graphics
Author Photo: Denise Aulie

ISBN: 978-0-692-32799-9

LCCN: 2014921758

Printed in USA

First Printing 2015

To every child:
You are a treasure and a blessing,
Worthy of love and protection.

Table of Contents

Foreword

by **Dr. Kathryn Wells**

Nationally recognized expert in Child Abuse Pediatrics

In a recent year, approximately 686,000 American children were abused or neglected, and almost 10 percent of those were victims of sexual abuse. In the vast majority of those cases the abuser was someone known to the child.

As a pediatrician who specializes in child abuse and neglect, I have dedicated my career to caring for children who suffer these atrocities. My passion is also to prevent these things from occurring. That is why Detective Diane Obbema's book, *Protecting Innocence*, is so important.

The most impactful way to prevent children from becoming victims of sexual abuse is to create parental awareness. *Protecting Innocence* helps arm parents and their children with the knowledge and life skills needed to maximize safety, deter predators, and keep vital parent-child communication open.

In her book, Detective Diane masterfully uses her extensive knowledge and firsthand experience of investigating child sexual assault cases to equip parents and caregivers with the understanding, language, and skills needed to better protect the children they care about.

In *Protecting Innocence*, readers will learn to identify situations that can pose increased risks to children; discover how to build crucial trust with their children; utilize the keys to building confidence in children; comfortably discuss sexual safety without jeopardizing a child's innocence; and know what to do if their child is victimized. Detective Diane skillfully and compassionately calls upon her wealth of experiences to provide practical approaches to the prevention of child sexual abuse.

I will enthusiastically recommend this book to colleagues as well as my own loved ones.

Kathryn Wells, MD, FAAP is Medical Director of the Denver Health Clinic at the Family Crisis Center in Colorado. She is Attending Physician at Denver Health and Children's Hospital, as well as Clinical Researcher at the world-renowned Kempe Center for the Prevention and Treatment of Child Abuse and Neglect. Dr. Wells is Associate Professor at the University of Colorado Department of Pediatrics.

Introduction

Many parents assume their children will talk to them about anything, but when faced with unexpected pressures involving their safety, children's fears can drive them into silence. Does your child have the confidence, and the know-how, to resist someone who wants to harm him or her? Would your child tell you if a trusted person committed a sexual violation against him or her? Most child victims do not tell … and if they do, not until years later.

In *Protecting Innocence* I will help you discover ways to keep communication with your child open regarding the most private of topics. This book will enable you to have meaningful conversations with your child about a subject he or she *needs* to know about: sexual safety.

I am Diane Obbema, a 30-year veteran of law enforcement. For 12 years I specialized as a detective in the Crimes Against Children Unit for the Jefferson County Sheriff's Office in Colorado. Many kids just know me as Detective Diane. My perspective in this book, as we explore issues and share common-sense defenses, is as a veteran detective. I have investigated hundreds of childhood sexual abuse cases through the years—interviewing victims, parents, and perpetrators—and it has given me a unique understanding of the many things involved in this type of crime.

National child abuse statistics show that 93% of child sexual abuse victims know their molesters in some way, and 68% are abused by family members. The odds are that the danger to your child's innocence would most likely come from someone *you* know personally.

In this book I will discuss important factors inside and outside the home that leave children vulnerable, and offer suggestions that can deter victimization. I will use real-life examples from my own cases, presenting you with first-hand insight into child molesters—how they think, and the tactics they use to seduce both parent and child. The true stories and time-tested advice will help you recognize relational red flags that indicate potential threats to your child. I place an emphasis on ways to build a deeper trust with your child to counter the methods that offenders use to undermine the vitally important parent-child bond.

After more than a decade of investigating child sexual abuse cases, I will share with you answers to these questions: *Can a child be sexually assaulted over years and no one know about it? Wouldn't an abused child show signs of abuse that others would notice? Can a child's word be trusted over an adult's? Can a child be close with others yet never trust them with a secret about being hurt? Why wouldn't a child tell?*

To protect children, parents must be willing to engage their children in meaningful, effective conversations that promote an open rapport and lay a foundation of trust.

As parents uncover their children's fears they must learn how to address those fears adequately.

This book will help parents learn ways to counter-punch the intimidation and manipulation tactics molesters employ to keep children from speaking out. Along the way I will share with you how to have four vital conversations with your children to build their confidence in healthy boundaries and maximize their protection from would-be offenders. And to help instill a surety in your home that they can always talk to you, should anyone threaten their safety.

Protecting Innocence identifies the communication skills every parent and caregiver needs to effectively discuss sexual safety with his or her young child. You will move past the discomfort of addressing these topics and learn to deal with them in a tactful and age-appropriate way, without the fear of corrupting your child's innocence. *Protecting Innocence* offers helpful terminology, wise talking-points, and practical "how-to" steps to maximize clear communication and minimize discomfort between you and your child.

It is my desire to empower you as a loving parent to confidently make a preemptive strike against any potential victimization of your child. You are your child's most important teacher and advocate. This book is a guide to impart wisdom and instill confidence, so your child can identify and resist potentially harmful situations. You will be able to build a trust with your child that no predator can easily break—and gain the assurance that your child *will* talk to you!

A few things to note regarding *Protecting Innocence*:

- This book's information is geared to parents with children who are 3-10 years old.

- The term "parent(s)" is frequently used within the text. However, this book is also intended for single parents, grandparents, and anyone who assumes a parental role with a child. Childcare providers, teachers, healthcare professionals, social workers, therapists, and law enforcement officers will also find the text insightful.

- My "voice"—Detective Diane's conversations— with child victims and molesters all come from real cases. Names have been changed to protect the victims' identities.

- Child molesters are referred to in the masculine gender. Female sexual offenders do exist, but they are relatively few in number. The cautions shared in this book apply to any person who interacts with your child, regardless of gender.

- Adults—who were victims of childhood sexual abuse—could find parts of this book disturbing. If so, please talk about it with a trusted friend, or seek the counsel of a qualified therapist.

A Child's Outcry

I drew the short straw among the Crimes Against Children detectives in December 1999. Having the on-call duty meant my family, all of whom lived out of state, would not be seeing my face at Christmas dinner. They would miss their chance to live vicariously through my animated retelling of the true crimes I'd been investigating the previous year. They knew I made an interesting guest at holiday parties once people knew my profession.

Being single meant it wasn't unusual for me to be assigned to work during the holidays. My many years in patrol gave me plenty of time to celebrate holidays inside my patrol car. But this year, as a detective, I anticipated a quiet, uneventful week. After all, it was Christmas!

I couldn't have been more wrong. Little did I realize events that week would prove to be the turning point in the lives of four small children. It started when eleven-year-old Cindy was watching a nightmare unfold.

Standing amidst twinkling lights and vibrantly colored packages, Cindy swallowed hard. A gripping fear stopped her in her tracks. Cindy's eyes were fixed on her mother,

Karen, marching up the stairs with Cindy's three-year-old sister, Mariah, in tow. Tiny Mariah looked like a rag doll being jerked along step-by-step by her tall, brooding mother. Cindy's face flushed and her heart pounded as she watched the two figures fade into the darkness at the top of the stairs. A bedroom door slammed shut … and the screaming began.

This was supposed to be a happy Christmas. It was Cindy and her three younger siblings' first overnight stay with mom and stepfather since being placed into foster care three months earlier. Grandma was the designated "supervisor" for this holiday visit. For whatever reason, that night Grandma turned a blind eye to what was happening, ignoring the one rule everyone was aware of: *no children were to be left alone with Mom.*

Cindy was accustomed to being the scapegoat for her mother's anger. Perhaps tonight was different because Karen knew the authorities were watching Cindy's well-being. Over the years Cindy's bruises, bumps, and black eyes had resulted in all the children going into foster care three separate times. Karen couldn't risk getting another criminal summons and court appearance. Tonight, Karen decided to focus her anger in another direction.

Cindy heard Mariah's cries finally subside. Karen emerged from upstairs to join the family now gathered around Grandma's cheerfully decorated table. Everyone assumed the "nothing's wrong" facade. They quickly began passing the turkey and all its fixings. Ingrained hyper-vigilance kept Cindy monitoring her mother's movements and mood. Thoughts plagued Cindy: "Was Mariah okay? Did Mariah have bruises? Would mom blame the bruises on Mariah's foster parents? What kind of lie would Mom want me to tell *this* time?"

Cindy knew her mother well. Long ago Cindy became proficient at repeating the lies her mother coached her to tell. To any inquiring minds, Karen wanted Cindy's injuries to be easily explained away. Falls on stairs, bicycle accidents, rough-housing with other kids, just being "clumsy," were common excuses. But some lies just didn't make sense. Repeated black eyes and knots on her forehead could no longer be attributed to "accidents." Someone noticed and called authorities. Cindy found herself being placed again, this time in the Camdens' foster home.

Cindy breathed a sigh of relief when she returned to Mike and Teri Camden's foster home after Christmas. The long, tense holiday visit was over. In a house full of children, foster mom Teri took time to have a private heart-to-heart conversation with the introverted Cindy. Helping Cindy unpack, Teri gently inquired about how things went during the visit.

"Okay," Cindy simply replied.

Teri's unconditional love for Cindy had built a bridge of trust over the prior three months, so it wasn't long before Cindy's concern for Mariah surfaced. Cindy told

Teri about Mariah being alone upstairs with their mom, and how she was afraid Mariah's foster parents might be blamed for any bruises Mariah had.

"No need to be afraid. I'll take care of it," Teri reassured. "Did anyone touch *you*?"

"No. No one touched me," said Cindy.

Several minutes passed as Cindy sat quiet. She silently weighed the risk of speaking any further. No one knew there was a deeper darkness in Cindy's life … and it didn't involve Mom.

"Teri," she finally ventured, "no one touched me during the visit, but someone has touched me before … my stepfather."

Looking straight ahead—as if speaking to no one—Cindy's secrets of sexual abuse by her stepfather began to be revealed. As if a dam had finally burst, Cindy poured out one horrific detail after another. Teri was careful to not interrupt, and quickly ushered out any child who ventured into the room. She listened intently while Cindy disclosed years of sexual abuse that started at age seven.

That night my phone rang. Stan, a child therapist from the Child Advocacy Center, informed me of Cindy's disclosure, what we call an "outcry." Stan and I agreed to interview Teri and Cindy the next morning.

When the shy eleven-year-old entered the room, I remember thinking how tiny she was for her age. Her small frame required her to frequently adjust the drooping shoulders of the oversized sweater she wore. We chatted about non-stressful topics so I could build a rapport, and assess where Cindy was developmentally. I learned Cindy was an artist at heart. She loved to read books and write poetry. Her excellent vocabulary showed Cindy to be an intelligent and introspective child. In the midst of her abuse, Cindy had found a degree of solace in the world of words.

Ever so gently, Stan and I began to ask questions about why she had come to see us. For over an hour in a soft voice that often was barely audible, Cindy disclosed years of sexual abuse by the only man she had known as a father. Cindy's recollection of sights, sounds, smells, and emotions painted a clear and frightening portrait of an isolated child who had no way out.

In Cindy's case I had no eyewitness, no DNA evidence, no photos or videos of the crime, and thanks to the step-father "lawyering up," I was given no chance to get a confession. I had no defining piece of evidence to convince a jury this crime happened.

For months I explored every avenue I could to obtain corroborating evidence that could substantiate or disprove the statements made by Cindy and others. Once I completed my investigation I knew exactly what to do.

I arrested Cindy's stepfather.

It took a year for me to have the opportunity to face this man in court. The long and difficult 10-day trial would leave a jury to decide his guilt.

Delayed Outcry

- 73% of child victims do not tell anyone about the abuse for at least a year.

- 45% of victims do not tell anyone for at least 5 years.

- Some never disclose.

The actual number of child sexual abuse victims is unknown, but the total is probably much higher due to lack of reporting.

(Sexual Assault Disclosure in Relation to Adolescent Mental Health: Results From the National Survey of Adolescents; Smith et al., 2000; Broman-Fulks et al., 2007)

Personal Notes

_____

_____

_____

_____

_____

_____

_____

_____

_____

_____

_____

_____

_____

_____

_____

_____

An Unpleasant Topic...
and a Childhood
Memory

Just using the words "child" and "sex" in the same sentence leaves a sick feeling in one's soul. The topic of child sexual abuse is disgusting. The acts are abhorrent. Just thinking about it can keep a parent up at night. Nobody, I mean nobody, is comfortable with this unpleasant topic.

One day I was discussing a case with a fellow Crimes Against Children (CAC) detective. We were in our cubicles at one end of the Investigations Unit. Suddenly I heard a detective from the Property Unit yell from the middle of the room. "Hey! You guys in CAC, keep it down! We don't want to hear about your cases!" I couldn't blame him. Who in their right mind wants to hear such details?

Even hardened veteran cops who have walked into bloody homicide scenes, separated domestic violence combatants, taken foul-mouthed drunks to detox, and handled gruesome traffic accidents, cringe when being dispatched to a child sexual abuse call.

But let us, as dispassionately as we can, discuss this most taboo of subjects. While my intention in writing this book is never to scare parents or fill your minds with horrible images, it is to educate truthfully. This book's importance rests on the understanding that children need their parents' help to be protected from danger that lurks in unexpected places, often very close to home.

Preparing you—to prepare your child—for the possibility of a predator's approach or presence means having a frank talk with you about things that might appear innocuous but possibly are not. There is no room for parents to put their heads in the sand simply because the topic of molestation is frightening or repulsive. Those who do are unwittingly putting their own children at risk.

"All that is necessary for the triumph of evil is that good men do nothing."
~ Edmund Burke

A child's world begins to expand within a few short years after birth. Whether it is preschool, Sunday school, sports, birthday parties, sleepovers, field trips, playing at a neighbor's house, or being left with a babysitter: growing children are increasingly out of parental view and interacting with others. Even though parents recognize that they cannot be with their children and protect them 24/7, their protective love naturally produces an uneasiness in seeing their children start to venture into new territories, beyond their protective watch.

Many years ago, I watched my three-year-old nephew Nathan while his parents were out of town. The weight of responsibility I felt was daunting. Here was this little human life … all in my care. I held his hand as we navigated the crowds of parents dropping their children off at Sunday school.

Once he was signed in, I let go of his hand. Nathan looked up at me with trusting eyes as I stepped away to go to church in another part of the building, all the while assuring him I would be back to get him.

This little boy I cherished slowly began mingling with others. Thoughts ran through my mind: "Will he be okay? Will they be nice to him? What if somebody hurts him?" Walking away brought an ache in the pit of my stomach. For the next hour he would not be in my direct care, but in the care of others. The thought was unnerving. I don't think I heard a word of the sermon that day.

But when I was a child, an even sicker feeling came over me.

The street I grew up on was filled with kids. We'd play all day and into the night during the summer (or at least until the street lights came on). Hide and Go Seek, Red Rover, Mother May I?, Red Light/Green Light, Cowboys and Indians, Freeze Tag. We had great fun! There was

17

rarely a fight amongst us, but when there was, it invariably involved one particular kid.

Micky was a year or so younger than I. He had a great imagination and often woke up the neighborhood early on Saturday mornings with the sound of a cavalry charge, running down the street. Micky lived next door to me and most of us kids knew he was troubled. Sometimes Micky would suddenly fly into a fit of blind rage when something didn't go his way. His behavior included yelling at the top of his lungs, throwing things, and stomping around in circles! It left us stunned, frozen with our mouths open, to see Micky's bizarre and inappropriate behavior. In a typical childlike reaction, we nicknamed him, and began referring to him as "Crazy Micky."

None of us realized that Micky had a lot of reasons to be "crazy."

One day I was shooting basketballs in my back yard. My attention was drawn away when I heard Micky's and his father's voices coming from the open window of Micky's bedroom. I could hear Micky pleading, "No, I don't want to. I don't want to." He was sobbing, "Please don't make me!" Each supplication was swiftly answered with the unmistakable smack of a hand hitting him—over and over again. It was terrifying to listen to Micky's father beating him.

I did the only thing a child could do in those days. I went into my house and told my mom. She stood at the stove stirring something she was preparing for dinner. Her response was typical for her generation: "Come inside. Close the door. We have to mind our own business."

So I did what I was told. Slowly I shut the back door, effectively drowning out Micky's cries. Yet I could not quiet the terrible aching in my heart, living with the painful knowledge that I could do nothing to help Crazy Micky.

Micky was sexually abused by his father for years. Micky had reasons for his rage.

I didn't know what child sexual abuse was back then. Nobody talked about it. No one recognized the signs. No one intervened. Consequently, it came as no surprise, years later, when I found out that Micky had sexually molested a little boy on our block.

Common Excuses Adults Give For Not Reporting Child Abuse

"I don't want to get involved."

"It might make matters worse."

"Family members will be angry at me."

"It might ruin my relationship with (the abuser) or (victim)."

"Someone else will speak up and do something."

"I can let my family (or church) handle it."

Those were innocent and ignorant times. People like my mom could not fathom child sexual abuse happening— certainly not by their fine, respectable, middle-class neighbor. These types of evils were not talked about on TV back then, or headlined in newspapers, or written about in parenting books. Famous pediatrician Dr. Benjamin Spock made no mention of it in his 1946 bestselling book, *Baby and Child Care*, the child-rearing bible for succeeding generations.

Times are very different now. Risks are higher. If we are to help children become wise and remain safe we need to invest in *all* aspects of their being; even discussing the uncomfortable topic of sexual safety.

Personal Notes

_____

_____

_____

_____

_____

_____

_____

_____

_____

_____

_____

_____

_____

_____

_____

_____

3

Protecting the Whole Child

Today's parents need to be wiser than previous generations of parents. All aspects of a child's humanity need to be attended to. Although today's parents meet their children's basic needs for food and shelter, and will actively involve their children in school, sports, the arts, and church, the topic of sexuality is still often neglected. Why? It's because the topic is uncomfortable, inconvenient, or viewed as unnecessary by parents.

The other morning, on my way to work, I made my usual stop at the Conoco station near my home. Despite years of attempts by my family to reform me, I still cannot shake my vice—diet soda—and I needed my daily fix that morning. As I filled my cup, I spotted a kindergartener with her young mother. I love to strike up conversations with children, so I asked the mother if I could give my law enforcement "trading card" to her daughter. Having received Mom's permission, I leaned down and introduced myself to little Bailey.

I wore my Class A uniform, the same as in the photo on my trading card. I talked to her about "yucky" feelings we can get in our "tummy" when something happens that we don't like. I pointed out to Bailey the Safety Tip that I put on the back of my card: "Don't keep quiet about someone hurting you. Tell an adult you trust." I suggested that her mom or teacher would be good people to talk to if something bothered her. Bailey smiled and took the card. Bailey's mom smiled and thanked me.

I went about my business, paying for my gas and diet soda. As I walked to my car, Bailey's mom approached to ask if she could have my phone number to call me later. She had "some questions" she wanted to ask. I gave her my business card and told her to call any time.

Help In Your Local Area

Many city and county agencies, and non-profit organizations, provide educational programs on many child safety issues:

- Seat belt safety
- Fire safety
- Water safety
- School and bus safety
- Internet safety
- Bicycle safety
- Home safety

For help, contact the Community Relations office in these local organizations:

- Police Department
- Sheriff's Office
- Fire Department
- Children's hospital
- Child Advocacy Center
- School district

Many major corporations sponsor child safety programs in their community. Check their websites for information.

This is a familiar scenario for me. Many times a mother has questions after hearing me talk to her child or teach a workshop. I believe Bailey's mom had a concern and would most likely ask about sexual issues. She might know a victim, or want guidance in handling a situation, or feel uncertain about how to talk about sexual predators, or perhaps she wanted me to address this issue to a PTA or women's group. Across the board, mothers worry about these things! Dads do, too, but moms do especially, and they welcome any help they can get.

But Bailey's mom never called. She might have become sidetracked by a demanding schedule or felt her questions were not that important after all. If she second-guessed herself on the validity of her concerns, she was wrong.

The saying, "the best defense is a good offense," is true for every aspect of a child's nurturing and training. What a full-time job this is! Here are some of the "Parenting 101" aspects we all know, but don't always consciously recognize.

Taking The Offense

Physically—Before danger has a chance to harm their children, parents should impart the wisdom of safety rules. From "look both ways" to "don't play with matches," to "never take candy from a stranger," safety rules help children recognize danger and to know the safest choice to make.

Intellectually—Parents should teach children colors, numbers, shapes, and letters. Educational books, toys, and games are sought after tools to help a child get ahead. Today, with more than 15 networks designed solely to entertain and expand your child's learning, children's television programming has advanced way beyond the borders of *Sesame Street*.

Socially—Beyond saying "please" and "thank you," parents should teach children which behaviors are appropriate and inappropriate in the social settings of family, friends, and community. They want their children to successfully interact with others and become respectful and responsible citizens.

Emotionally—Parents should foster a child's positive attachment to them through tender care and affection. With parental guidance children begin to identify good and bad feelings, learn that emotions are okay, and that everyone has them. Parents demonstrate through example and wise words the different ways children can properly express their feelings, especially the more difficult emotions such as anger and frustration.

Spiritually—Parents should impart beliefs to children, truths that lay a moral foundation, so children become persons of admirable character, desiring to choose right over wrong. Belief in a loving God and the value of humanity will motivate children to cherish their own lives and those of others.

Parents have so much to do in raising and shaping healthy, happy children. But did you notice an aspect of a child's personhood missing from this list? There is one. It's "Sexually." There it is—that uncomfortable topic.

Children are male or female. Their gender is an intrinsic part of who they are. Looking out for children's total well-being includes caring for and protecting their sexual natures.

Child Sexual Abuse

Of the child sexual abuse victims reported in 2012, one-third (33.8%) were younger than 9 years and 26.3 percent were in the age group of 12–14 years.

(*Child Maltreatment 2012 Report*, National Child Abuse and Neglect Data System, U.S. Dept. of Health and Human Services)

44% of rapes with penetration occur to children under age 18. Victims younger than 12 accounted for 15% of those raped, and another 29% of rape victims were between 12 and 17.

(National Crime Victimization Survey, 2002, U.S. Dept. of Justice, Bureau of Justice Statistics)

Only about 38% of child victims disclose the fact that they have been sexually abused.

(London, K., Bruck, M., Ceci, S. J., & Shuman, D. W. (2005). Disclosure of child sexual abuse: What does the research tell us about the ways that children tell? *Psychology, Public Policy, & Law, 11*, 194-226.)

My mother gave birth to three daughters. In her fourth pregnancy, she and my father—although longing for a boy—prepared to welcome another little girl into the family. At that time there were no tests or ultrasounds available to determine the baby's gender before birth. So as my father paced the waiting room (as all fathers did then), my mother was pushing away to deliver her next daughter.

When the baby arrived the doctor excitedly announced, "It's a boy!" My mother gave him a stern look and a prompt rebuke. "That is a cruel joke!" she said. The doctor's word was definitely not good enough. So lifting my brother in the air with his umbilical cord still attached, the doctor happily proclaimed, "The plumbing is on the outside!" Seeing was believing. My mother sent the nurses to tell my father. His excitement soon echoed down the hospital's hallway. He had a son!

Gender has its hallmarks. There is the predominance of different hormones: estrogen or testosterone; and different chromosomes, XX or XY. Certain body parts and their functions are uniquely male or female. "Plumbing," as the doctor noted, is on the inside or outside. So when it comes to educating children about sexual safety, there is a need to talk about differences between the sexes.

Children who have seen a younger sibling, or a baby of the opposite sex without clothes, probably have already noticed gender differences. More than likely, the child pointed out the difference to the parent, along with a question or two. Interesting and humorous questions can be posed at the oddest times, like when guests were over, or while at church, or when shopping at the mall. The nervous, embarrassed parent often responds with a quick, simple answer, "We'll talk about that later," or "Boys and girls are different," or "We don't talk about those things in public." Silently, the parent hopes the answer will satisfy the child's curiosity; and the parent will not be subjected to the dreaded follow-up questions: "Why?", "How come?", or "What does it do?"

This reminds me of a scene in the movie *Kindergarten Cop*, when a little boy stands up and proudly informs his new teacher, "Boys have a penis and girls have a vagina." The awkwardness of the moment is what makes the scene so funny. We aren't used to hearing sex-related words coming from a child. And we sure don't want to explain those words.

Out of our own discomfort, we often revert to nicknames and euphemisms. Mr. Peter, chi-chi, woo-woo, family jewels, cookies, hoo-hoo, fluff, cuchie … the list goes on and on. Through years of conducting child forensic interviews, I've heard a variety of names given to male and female genitalia… pretty humorous ones, too. Parents pass down nicknames they heard from their parents, who probably heard it from their parents. (Who would have thought genealogy was associated with the naming of private parts?) Yet for many of us, our parents passed on more than just cutesy names; they passed on their discomfort about addressing sexually related issues.

To the parent who feels squeamish at the thought of saying words like "penis" and "vagina" to a three-year-old, let me say I understand. As adults, we automatically equate those terms with sex. But let me put you at ease, I am not suggesting children need details about sex to be educated about sexual safety. Knowing the term for a body part is one thing. Knowing *all the function*s of that body part is something else. There is no need to introduce or explain sexual acts to young children. It's enough for them to learn that their bodies are special, with every part having an important (non-sexual) job to do.

You might be thinking to yourself: "Why should I introduce anatomically correct terms to my child? Isn't that unnecessary? I'd rather use a code word that isn't so embarrassing to say in public." Teaching children the proper names for sexual body parts has definite advantages in furthering their safety. I'll share why and we'll look at some easy ways to accomplish this in the next chapter.

Protecting children from sexual predators begins with being on the same page—language-wise—with our children. This not only helps the parent, but it helps police, medical professionals, teachers, therapists, clergy, and others who, by law, are mandated to report abuse. In Colorado, as elsewhere in the country, mandated persons must report all *known or suspected* child abuse to either local law enforcement or Child Protective Services. Important intervention can take place quickly if children can clearly communicate to a trusted adult exactly what has happened to them.

What Was It Like For You?

What is your family's code name for private parts?

Why do you think those names were chosen?

How did your parents handle questions about sexuality?

Is there something you wish they had done different?

Discuss these questions with your spouse, too.

Personal Notes

4

The Proper Names for Intimate Parts

A four-year-old girl once told me she had been touched in China. It took a few minutes and some clarifying questions before I understood that she had not been to China. Rather, she was touched in her "china." It made a world of difference when I figured out "china" was the child's word for vagina.

The momentary confusion gave me pause, but had I not clarified that this child was indeed referring to her vagina, the case on her behalf would have suffered. Defense lawyers would have had a field day arguing that the child never disclosed being touched in an intimate area, as the law requires to be proved. The defense might argue that the prosecution did not have jurisdiction because the alleged crime occurred in … you guessed it—China!

To file a criminal case, a detective must present information that supports the charge to the district attorney's office. A detective cannot give vague speculation on what *might have* happened to the child. The use of family nicknames, crude slang, or double entendres only confuses the issue. If children know the proper names for intimate body parts, they are more likely to clearly explain what has happened to them. Teaching children anatomically correct names enables them to identify which parts of their bodies have been inappropriately touched. Referring to "down there" is far too ambiguous.

"Penis," "bottom," "vagina," and "breast" are basic terms children should know and use when referring to their intimate parts. As a parent, if you are *not* comfortable using those terms, I have some advice: for the sake of your child, it's time to get over it. Why? Because your child will read you like a book.

If parents can't be comfortable using these words, then their children will not be comfortable either. Worse, a child could interpret a parent's discomfort as an indication that these body parts are somehow "dirty" or bad. If something were to happen to those parts, the child would be less likely to tell that parent about the abuse. Children will choose to be silent rather than say something they think will upset a parent.

If the home environment allows jokes or crude comments about sex or private parts, the body's importance is openly degraded. Children are less likely to talk about sexual abuse if they suspect that doing so puts them at risk of being humiliated by those closest to them. Instead, they will keep silent. Children need parents to demonstrate by word, action, and attitude that the human body is a good thing—*every* part of the body is good.

The point here is: parents who want their children to talk to them must be approachable. Children who feel secure—knowing no subject is off limits with mom or dad—are more likely to talk about what has happened to them.

Parents can build a bridge with their children on the topic of sexual safety by using anatomically correct terms in a matter-of-fact, respectful way. No drama, no shame or embarrassment, just straightforward language. Learning "penis," "bottom," "vagina," and "breasts" is easiest if parents start using the terms as children learn the names of other body parts. If a child has already learned nicknames for these parts, it's not too late for parents to introduce and use the proper terms now.

There are some simple steps to teach anatomically correct names to your child. (The following example refers to a boy, but applies to girls also.)

How To Teach The Proper Names For Intimate Parts

1. Begin by sharing with your child just how special he is. *"It is great to be a boy!"* Remind him how you love him and always want him to be safe. Say, *"Your body is a very important part of you. There are things we do to care for and protect our special bodies."*

2. Point out that properly caring for our bodies involves many things: *"Feeding our bodies the right foods helps us will grow big and strong … washing our bodies keeps us clean and protects us from getting sick … wearing clothes protects us from being too cold or too hot … respecting our bodies means we treat our bodies in the right way so we don't get hurt."*

3. Tell your child that some body parts are to be kept private: *"One of the ways we respect our bodies is by covering the parts that are private. We take extra care with these private parts by covering them with our underwear or our bathing suit. We don't show these parts to other people because they are private. Other people are not to show us their private parts."*

4. Explain the gender similarities and differences in private parts: *"Boys have private parts, and girls have private parts. Some private parts are the same, and some are different. Boys and girls both have bottoms. We sit on our bottoms and that is where we go pooh. Each boy has a private part called a penis. Boys use their penises to go pee.*

   Now, each girl has a private part called a vagina. The vagina is an opening between a girl's legs that is covered by two flaps of skin. The vagina is near the area where girls go pee. Girls also have breasts that get bigger as they grow up. Breasts can hold milk for newborn babies." (In order to avoid confusion, I don't think it is necessary to teach small children words like scrotum, anus, or labia. But the choice is yours. Testicles might not be an essential body part for girls to learn, but boys should know it.)

Using simple drawings of an anatomically correct male and female child can be very helpful during this discussion. (See example drawings in the back of book.) You or your child can point to a body part, and your child can name it. Knowing the general function of certain private parts helps distinguish one private part from another. Many children will say that the vagina is "where a girl goes pee," and that is sufficient. It is important to have your child repeat the name of each part so you hear the child's pronunciation of the word. Some children have speech difficulties. If penis is pronounced "eemis," that's fine. You just want to clearly know what your child is referring to if the word is used.

Conveying The Information

A friendly, caring, and matter-of-fact delivery of this information can result in a more knowledge-able and confident child. Such a child is less likely to be targeted for abuse.

Please note that these anatomical drawings should only be used by you during a private conversation with your child. The drawings should not be considered pictures for coloring, nor put on the shelf next to *Thomas the Train* and *Hello, Kitty*. After use, put the drawings away in a secure place for later use during "refresher" conversations (about six months later.) Anatomical drawings should only be used by parents when teaching the names of private parts. Parents should not use them to question a child about sexual abuse.

A forensic interviewer is the only one trained to use anatomical drawings in determining if sexual abuse has occurred. Good forensic interviewing means letting the child define what occurred. Interviewers must remain neutral, and never assume or suggest answers. Forensic interviewers receive more complete and accurate information by asking children *non-leading* questions. A good question is one that does not lead the child towards a particular answer.

Children are impressionable and can often take cues from the adults around them. If a question is not asked properly, a child might offer an answer according to what the child *thinks* the adult wants to hear. A child might change an answer if a question is asked too many times. By asking non-leading questions the child has opportunity to volunteer information he or she personally knows.

Non-leading questions often begin with who, what, when, and where.

A *leading* question is one that is presented in such a way that it suggests a certain answer to the child; or one that makes assumptions about facts yet to be confirmed. Leading questions can often be answered by "yes" or "no." To make a statement, and then follow it with a question that asserts an answer, is leading the child. Let's say your child comes home with a scrape on his face. A leading question would be: "Jerry was mean to you today, right?" You have led the child to agree with your assumption. Non-leading questions would be: "Who were you playing with today? What things did you do? How did you boys get along? What caused that scrape on your face?"

Sometimes well-meaning parents jeopardize a disclosure or a criminal case by asking too many questions before a trained interviewer can question the child. Anxious parents have difficulty remaining neutral when it comes to the suspected abuse of their child. This anxiousness can result in questions being asked in the wrong way. There should be a limited number of questions a parent asks a child who reports sexual abuse. There will be more on this subject in Chapter 12.

Young Children And False Allegations

It is rare, but in some cases a forensic interviewer will detect that a child had been influenced or coached by someone regarding an allegation of sexual abuse. Young children do not tend to lie about sexual abuse. If they lie, it is usually due to an outside influence.

One time I conducted a forensic interview with a little boy who had not been taught the proper names for his intimate parts. He told me a neighbor had touched his "private." I could not assume he was referring to a sexual area of his body. I took him through a body part inventory using an anatomical drawing of a little boy. He named multiple parts and told me their functions, such as "eyes help us see," "ears help us hear," "a nose is for smelling," "arms lift things up," and "hands wave goodbye."

When we came to the penis and bottom, he referred to both as "private." To clarify further I asked what those parts did. The little guy was too embarrassed to tell me. (Some children will say, "I don't know," rather than mention "pooh" or "pee.") I told him that since there were two places named "private," I might not understand which one he was talking about. I asked if there was some way we could tell the two privates apart. He pointed to the penis in the drawing and said that was the "front private." Then he pointed to the bottom calling it the "back private." I then put the drawings away. Using the designations he had given for each private, I was able to clearly understand which part of his body he was referring to as the forensic interview continued. If this boy had learned proper anatomical names and functions, with no associated embarrassment, he would have been able to describe what occurred sooner with more clarity.

Parents can encourage a child's self-worth and self-respect by conveying the message that every part of the child's body is important, needs to be taken care of, and deserves to be respected by others. Give your child a sense of ownership by telling him or her, *"Your body belongs to you. You are in charge of your body. Others should respect you and treat you the right way. If anything happens to your body that you don't like, I want you to come and tell me about it. I won't be upset with you."* If children can talk about intimate body parts with a parent now, in a calm, no-shame environment, they are more likely to talk about any uncomfortable situations later.

Remember, the parent's demeanor sets the tone for the conversation. If you are embarrassed, your child will feel something is wrong when talking about these things. If you are silly and make a joke of things, your child won't take it seriously. A friendly, caring, and matter-of-fact delivery of this information can result in a more knowl-edgeable and confident child. Such a child is less likely to be targeted for abuse.

Respect For Our Bodies

Parents can encourage a child's self-worth and self-respect by conveying the message that *every part of the child's body:*

- is important
- needs to be taken care of
- deserves to be respected by others.

In the first chapter of this book I told you about Cindy. As an 11 year-old, Cindy already knew the anatomical names of male and female genitalia from her "Growing and Changing" class at school. Yet when she first described her sexual abuse to her foster mother, Cindy used the term "his thing" when referring to her stepfather's penis. Using this euphemism demonstrated Cindy's embarrassment in discussing the topic. Cindy used this same term the following day in my interview with her. I asked Cindy what "his thing" meant. Cindy said, "his penis." I asked what a penis was. Cindy said, "the boy's thing between the legs." When asked what a penis was used for, Cindy replied, "peeing."

These non-leading questions clarified for me (and later, for the District Attorney) that Cindy was referring to her stepfather's penis when using the term "his thing." My relaxed use and acceptance of the word "penis" helped Cindy feel more comfortable. As the interview progressed, Cindy began to use the more specific term "penis" when telling me what her stepfather did.

My level of comfort with sexual terms, and my non-judgmental acceptance of the details she was sharing, helped Cindy communicate difficult details more freely. By knowing the proper names for sexual body parts, Cindy could clearly explain to me the different sexual assaults she had suffered. Though Cindy detailed horrible acts, I did not respond emotionally—not in my words, or tone, or facial expressions. I calmly listened, gave Cindy good eye contact, and followed up with my next non-leading questions.

Being on the same page—language-wise—is essential for better communication between parent and child. If you take the time to teach your child the proper names for privates, he or she will be less embarrassed to discuss any issue that might involve those parts of the body.

Leading vs. Non-Leading Questions

A **leading** question is one that is presented in such a way that it suggests a certain answer to the child; or one that makes assumptions about facts yet to be confirmed. Leading questions can often be answered by "yes" or "no."

In everyday life, parents wanting to know more about a situation involving their child should practice asking **non-leading** questions. You will get the most accurate and unbiased information through the non-leading question because the child has opportunity to volunteer information he or she personally knows. Non-leading questions are not presumptive or accusatory. Non-leading questions do not assume or project your own opinion, thus allowing you to get more information directly from your child. Non-leading questions often begin with who, what, when, and where.

A non-leading question does not suggest an answer.

Example situation: Child comes home from school.

Leading: You had a good day at school today, huh?

Non-leading: What happened at school today? Tell me all about it.

A non-leading question does not contain a choice of answers.

Example situation: You find the TV was left on all night.

Leading: Did you or your brother leave the TV on all night?

Non-leading: When did you go to bed last night? Who was watching TV after you?

A non-leading question does not identify a person before the child has identified him/her.

Example situation: Money is missing off the table.

Leading: Sean took the money off the table, didn't he?

Non-leading: Who has been in the house today? Where did the money on the table go? When did you last see it?

Personal Notes

Choosing Protective Boundaries for Your Home

This chapter might not sit well with some parents, but that's okay. After years of listening to tragic things that happened behind closed doors, I cannot pull any punches. Here's my challenge: for the sake of your child, look with a critical eye at *how you conduct yourself* and *what you allow within your own home.*

Boundaries are markers, set to define limits. These dividing lines help children identify what is acceptable and what is not. A boundary is saying to your child: "Our family will behave in certain ways that protect what we value." For example, if cursing is not allowed in the home, that is a boundary. It teaches children that speaking respectfully to others is a value within the family; therefore, disrespectful words are unacceptable. Parents who adhere to this boundary in their own lives lead by example, and foster the value of respect within their child's character. Of course, the opposite will also be true.

The cursing parent sabotages the message of respect. Children see the hypocrisy in "do as I say and not as I do." Respect becomes a joke, not a value.

Healthy boundaries practiced within the home reinforce the message to children that *each person's **body** needs to be respected.* Sadly, some parents permit practices that undermine this vital message.

Parents who believe that sexually explicit images are inappropriate and harmful for small children to see must think seriously about the presence of pornography in their own homes. Network television programming might still have *some* standards, but many cable channels do not. Displays of adult male and female frontal nudity and explicit sexual acts are available on many cable stations. Parents who don't think children know how to use a remote control, a DVD player, a computer, or a smart phone are kidding themselves. Children and teens can access pornography if it is available. Hiding porn for private viewing is no guarantee it won't be discovered. I know this because many children have told me they have viewed it and where their parents' stashes were located.

The younger children are exposed to content intended for adults in television and movies, the earlier they become sexually active during adolescence."
(Boston Children's Hospital, 2009 study)

Curiosity is part of a child's make-up. So, too, is parroting the actions and behaviors that children observe. Graphic sexual images available through TV shows, DVDs, cell phones, websites, lap tops, iPads, computer files, thumb drives, magazines, song lyrics, or photographs provide information and images a child is neither prepared to understand nor able to cope with on any level—mental, emotional, psychological, physical, or spiritual.

Viewing such images can become a catalyst for a child to act out sexually. Every teenage sex offender I have interviewed had pornography as part of his life—every single one! When these boys viewed porn, curiosity and sexual arousal set in and took over! These boys started acting out with the only victims they had access to: younger children. The victims included siblings, cousins, neighborhood children, daycare kids, etc. All of these innocent children became victims of teens inspired by pornography.

I am not talking about innocent interaction between very young children who might be "playing doctor." I am talking about teens *choosing* to molest others who are smaller and more vulnerable. Despite knowing that such actions would be wrong, they chose to offend; motivated to commit these crimes to achieve their own sexual gratification.

The youngest offender I ever arrested was a 12-year-old boy. I'll call him Kenny. He was a medium-framed, fair-haired boy with a round face, wearing wire-rimmed glasses that made him look studious. He was a real cutie and quite precocious. With his parents' permission, Kenny and I spoke about his relationship with his younger sister and brother, ages 5 and 3, respectively (I had already interviewed the siblings). Kenny had a typical older-brother view of having to tolerate his siblings.

When I mentioned the things his siblings talked about, Kenny became uncomfortable. His first response was to dismiss their statements as being from "their imaginations." My details were specific enough for Kenny to realize his siblings spilled the beans. There was no way he could bluff his way out of this situation. Eventually, Kenny started telling the truth. He told me how he sexually violated his sister and brother. These abuses happened on multiple occasions over several months. This happened at his home while his parents were in other rooms.

"How did you get the idea to do these things?" I asked.

"Well," he replied frankly, "I just put in the word 'playboy' in the search part on the computer."

Kenny visited several sites and explained to me how he saw photos of naked women. He noticed a portion of one webpage that highlighted the "sex tip of the day." He followed the link. He liked what he saw and read. It was titillating. Kenny told me he had erections while viewing these materials, and he would take every opportunity to be on the computer whenever his parents were not around. Soon it wasn't enough to just look at pictures, or try to imagine the acts that were so vividly described in print. Kenny decided to live out his fantasies by assaulting his vulnerable siblings. The assaults were followed by stern warnings from Kenny to his sister and brother, "Don't tell Mom or Dad!" Kenny told me he knew these acts were wrong, but he didn't care. I could see this. Kenny showed no remorse for his actions, nor empathy for the trauma that he caused his sister and brother.

I knew Kenny would offend again if given any opportunity. I sought out options for placing him with other family members who had no children, or in a foster home. But no one was willing, or available, to take him. So to insure his siblings' safety, I took custody of Kenny and placed him in a juvenile detention center. My hope was that with early intervention and specific counseling, Kenny could learn proper boundaries, gain empathy, and eventually be reunited with his family. I knew it would be a long process.

Kenny continued to struggle throughout his early teens. His name surfaced occasionally as the years passed, usually associated with a fight with other juveniles, but I wasn't assigned those cases and had no contact with him.

One day, my desk phone rang at headquarters. It was the deputy who provides security in the public lobby.

"Detective Obbema, do you know a Kenny _____?"

"Yes. I arrested him eight years ago."

"Well, he's down here in the lobby asking for you. I asked if he had an appointment with you. He said he didn't. Do you want to see him?"

"Sure. Tell him to have a seat. I'll be right down."

I hung up the phone and wondered, *"After all these years, why would he come see me? I'm surprised he even remembers my name."*

Kenny was taller, of course, wearing a black leather jacket and jeans. He had a couple of tattoos on his hands. His blonde hair had darkened, but his glasses were surprisingly similar to what he wore years earlier. He stood up as I approached him with my hand extended, "Hello, Kenny. How are you? It's been a long time." We shook hands, and he gave a slight smile. "Hello, Detective Obbema. I'm okay. I wanted to come see you."

I ushered him into a small office so we could talk privately. I started the conversation by telling him that I had often thought about the night we met. Kenny was surprised as I recalled personal things about him from that evening. "You really do remember!" he said. I shared how I wished there could have been a different option for placement that night, but I had to insure protection for his brother and sister.

"That's why I'm here." Kenny said, "I wanted to thank you. It stopped me from going down a wrong road. I would have hurt others. I just wanted you to know."

Digital And Internet Dangers

Over the last several years, the FBI, state and local law enforcement, and the public have developed an increased awareness of the child pornography/child sexual exploitation crime problem. More online incidents of these crimes are being identified for investigation than ever before. Between fiscal years 1996 and 2007, the number of cases opened throughout the FBI catapulted from 113 to 2,443. From 2007 to the present, the numbers have steadily continued to rise. In December 2013, the FBI had approximately 7,759 pending child pornography/child sexual exploitation investigations under this program. As the power and popularity of the Internet continue to expand, the number these cases opened will likely continue to grow.

(Federal Bureau of Investigation – Violent Crimes Against Children Program; www.fbi.gov)

What an unexpected blessing to see this young man. Cops rarely, if ever, get that kind of positive feedback. Kenny and I finished our time talking about his hopes for the future. He was still working on his family relationships, but he had a job and was getting married. He proudly showed me a picture of his fiancé. I asked him to give my regards to his parents. He said he would.

Such a long, hard struggle for this young man. How different life would have been for Kenny—and his siblings—if he had never seen pornography. Kenny's life is a cautionary tale. Pornography corrupts and confuses young minds.

Any device with an Internet connection is a potential gateway to pornography for your child. What filters do you have on those devices? Invest in a parent-recommended software program that gives you control over what your child can access. Protecting children and teens from viewing pornography should be a top priority of parents. Wise parents will give it no place in their home. This is a healthy boundary!

According to a March 2013 report by NPD Group, a global research company, the average U.S. household has 5.7 devices connected to the Internet. What your child can't access at your home he might access at a friend's home. It is always wise to know the parents of your child's friends. Initiating a discussion with them about this issue could help protect your child.

On a less graphic scale, other practices in the home can also undermine the respect-levels children should have for their bodies. Practices such as: parents who walk around the house nude; parents who shower or bathe with children old enough to care for their own hygiene; parents who leave doors open when dressing, using the restroom, or having sex; or parents who joke openly about sex, breasts, or genitalia—these are all examples of poor boundaries. These actions subvert the message of respect children should be learning: *You and your body are special. Your private parts are to be kept covered, and not viewed or touched by others. No one is to show you his or her private parts.*

Be The Media Gatekeeper

- View programs with your children.

- Select age-appropriate shows.

- Limit the amount of daily TV viewing and computer time.

- Place the TV/computer in family areas and not in individual bedrooms.

- No phones or tablets in children's rooms overnight.

- Turn off the TV/computer during family meal time.

- Turn off shows you don't feel are appropriate.

- Talk about the content of TV shows and movies. Share your reactions and beliefs about what is being portrayed.

My five-year-old niece was taking a bath one night. To check on her, I knocked on the bathroom door and announced myself. "Come in!" she shouted. I entered to see her actively moving around the tub. "Take a picture of me swimming, Aunt Diane!" She wanted her water adventures memorialized with my new camera. I told her I couldn't take a picture of her swimming because it would show her bottom. I reminded her, "Our privates are private." Without a hint of disappointment, she replied, "Oh, that's right." And she continued playing.

She and I had previous conversations about how to care for and respect our bodies. Keeping our privates covered was part of that discussion. What I practiced in my home (i.e. the door being closed while bathing, knocking on the door, announcing myself, asking permission to enter, and declining to take a photo of her naked) served to reinforce the lessons I taught her about respect. My niece is realizing her value. She is learning to expect respect from others. She also knows to speak up boldly should anyone not show her the respect she deserves.

We want our children to respect themselves. If you are teaching your child the behaviors, words, and attitudes that show respect, it will strike him or her as inappropriate when others act contrary. And that's a good thing.

Expect Respect

Share with your child ways that respect is shown to others. Let him know that children should be respected too!

- Listen without interrupting.

- Say what you need to say without yelling or name-calling.

- Use the words "please" and "thank you."

- Never ask someone to do something that would be embarrassing.

- Ask nicely. If someone says "no", accept it. Don't demand your own way.

- Compliment the nice things about a person.

- Only touch someone with "okay" touches.

- Say "I'm sorry" if you hurt someone's feelings.

- Be truthful.

- Never keep a secret about someone being hurt.

- Be kind, not mean. If someone is mean, tell that person, "That is not nice." Tell an adult you trust about it.

Ask your child, when he or she returns home from an event, if there was anything that made them free uncomfortable about how others acted. Your child's response might provide you with insight to influences you don't want your child around. You can then discuss with your child how being disrespected by others does not need to be tolerated. The selection of friends, activities, and environments should pass the respect-level test. All the while, parents must be demonstrating respect—particularly in regards to the human body – within their own home.

Teaching respect for one's privates means the *touching, viewing, or discussion of intimate parts* should always have a *legitimate purpose*. Walking around "in the buff" just because a dad wants to, or showering with children to "save time and water," do not constitute legitimate reasons for exposing adult or teen genitals to children. Parents who practice modesty demonstrate respect for the human body, and teach their children the proper behaviors to emulate.

A child needs to know that only *certain people,* for *specific reasons*, can see or touch the child's genitals. Parents should clarify who those people are and what circumstances allow for this. For example, a doctor might examine your child's private parts if your child is hurt in those places. You can assure your child that either Mom or Dad will always be present during the exam. If medicine is necessary, and the child cannot apply it, a parent or grandparent (preferably a female relative for girls) can apply it. Also, children can understand that babies are too small to take care of themselves. A baby's private parts may be touched by a caregiver during bathing or changing the baby's diapers. These are the only exceptions to the boundary that says, "No one can touch your private parts."

Young siblings or their friends who are in the house might gather around when a baby's diapers are being changed. If a child asks a question about a baby's body part, use it as a teachable moment. Remind the children that these parts are private and the only reason you are taking the baby's diaper off is to care for the baby's needs. Point out that they are older and can care for themselves. They need privacy when changing clothes or going to the bathroom because their privates should kept private. Go about your business changing the baby without lingering in a discussion.

One day I talked with a mother of a young sexual assault victim to better understand her family's attitude about intimate body parts. The mom mentioned it was common for extended family members to wiggle her infant son's penis and joke, "Don't worry, you'll grow up someday."

Perhaps no harm was intended, but I could not help but wonder what message this accepted behavior sent to other children in the family. The message might be that private parts are for others to touch when they want to; or touching privates is funny; or if people touch my little brother, it must be okay for someone to touch me; or it's okay for me to touch someone else's privates. Accepted family practices that *contradict* good boundaries make children vulnerable to becoming sexualized.

Establishing healthy boundaries within the home teaches a child to expect the same privacy and respect from others outside the home. Defining clear boundaries helps make a child wiser. It enables a child to have a keen internal alarm, which is set to go off should anyone step over the boundary the parent has discussed with the child.

A good way to label boundaries for children is by calling them "safety rules." By teaching safety rules, parents enable children to identify where the boundaries are set. Children can understand that when someone does not respect and obey a safety rule, something is wrong.

Parents can increase their child's sensitivity to danger (without causing undo fear) by discussing how the child's feelings will help protect him or her. Let your child know that uncomfortable or "yucky" feelings—like sad, mad, confused, embarrassed, scared, or a feeling they can't name—are helping the child to remember what to do: go to a safe place and talk with a safe person. Assure your child that talking with a safe person will help the "yucky" feelings go away.

Tell your child that if *any* person—family, friend or stranger—breaks a safety rule regarding touching or showing private parts, the child will have one of those uncomfortable feelings. Let your child know that you will always be ready to listen and help if this happens.

Children who have had clear and consistent examples of healthy boundaries within the home will recognize danger faster. They will be quicker to act on what they've been taught: *Move away from the danger as quickly as possible, find a trusted adult, and tell what happened.* It will be harder for a perpetrator to successfully cross a boundary if children react to the danger they *feel*. What children don't want—or need—is confusion about the human body's value or its purpose. Parents, let the attitudes and behaviors within your home reinforce to your children what is good, right, and respectable.

When Other Parents Don't Follow Your Safety Rules

Helping your child to know how to respond to adults who do not follow your family's safety rules is important. The safety rule may have nothing to do with touching. Perhaps there is an adult who is okay to let your child ride without a car seat, or swim without a life vest, or watch an R-rated movie. In these cases you will want your child prepared to speak up. Role-play with your child on how to respond in these situations *before* they happen. Here is some suggested wording for your child for the above examples:

Child: *"Mr. Brown, my parents told me that I must always sit in a car seat when I'm in a car. It's so I can stay safe. Is there one that I can use?"*

Child: *"Mrs. Smith, my parents say I cannot go swimming without wearing a vest. It is so I can stay safe. Is there one that I can borrow?"*

Child: *"Mr. Jones, my parents do not allow me to watch R-rated movies. Is there something else we can watch?"*

These responses help other adults understand that your child knows the boundaries you have given him; he respects your authority as his parent; and that it is likely your child will talk with you later about this situation.

Let your child know that he can call you anytime he feels he is in an uncomfortable situation. And that you will always be proud of his good decision to talk with you.

Honest communication with your child helps you better understand the environment he or she is in when away from home.

Personal Notes

6

"Okay" and "Not Okay" Touches

My family is an affectionate family. Our get-togethers are filled with hugs, grasping hands, interlocking arms, pats on the back, sitting next to each other, and many, many kisses for the little ones. We hug when arriving. We hug when leaving. It's just part of how we love each other. Other families might be more reserved in their displays of affection.

Human touch is a wonderful thing. As humans, we need touch to feel a sense of love, security, and belonging. Touch is also a powerful thing. *Where* touch happens, *when* it happens, *how* it happens, and *who* it happens with, can have an impact on us to the core of our being. Touch can leave lifelong imprints on our souls. Some imprints will be good and nurturing; tragically, some will be bad and horribly destructive.

How can children know what kind of touch is beneficial and what kind is destructive?

How children *feel* can certainly be a barometer, in some cases. A pat on the back makes them feel appreciated and proud. A handshake lets children know they are being acknowledged and welcomed. Those are good feelings. On the other hand, a kick in the shins or a punch on the arm does not feel good at all. Children would easily decipher that the latter touches belong in the "bad" category, because these touches hurt!

Assessing the right kind of touch by *feelings alone* can be misleading. To say, "good touches feel good" and "bad touches feel bad," is not enough information for a child. A shot from the doctor or a corrective swat away from a hot stove might not *feel* good at all. Touches that produce physical discomfort might be a good thing, and necessary to keep children healthy and safe. Conversely, bad touches might not always *feel* bad.

As adults we know that children are not responsible for their abuse, but children do not comprehend this on their own. Many will assume they did something wrong. Children can be conflicted in their feelings about the abuse because their bodies are experiencing something they were never intended to experience at this age … sexual contact.

Several boy victims I've interviewed felt guilty about their victimization. These boys felt a deep shame and a responsibility for what happened to them. Why? The reason was simple: the bad touching felt good to them. Even though they knew what was happening to them was wrong, their body had a pleasurable response to the sexual touching. This was very confusing to them. Whenever I saw this guilt in a child, I took the time to simply share how our bodies naturally respond to touch. "That's just how we're made," I'd say. "Your body responded automatically. So you did nothing wrong." This helped to alleviate the child's guilt and allowed the child to open up more about what occurred.

A better way to categorize "good" and "bad" touches for children is to label them "okay" and "not okay" touches. This way, children won't need to rely solely on their feelings to assess the presence of danger. Parents can help their children determine when a touch (that might or might not feel good) is a "not okay" touch by giving them examples. These concrete examples make the boundary even clearer to the child, because it describes an act, not just a feeling.

Here are some suggestions. (The example uses the feminine gender but applies to both boys and girls.)

1. Have this discussion in private. Select a time when you will not be distracted or interrupted. This one-on-one time will make your child feel special, and will emphasize the importance of what you have to share.

2. Ask your child: *"Can you tell me the safety rule for crossing the street?"* or *"What is the safety rule about matches?"* Listen to the responses.

Praise your child for the correct answer. Say, *"Today I want to talk about safety rules for touching. These rules are very important because you and your body are very important."*

3. Let your child know there are different types of touches. Some touches are "okay" and some are "not okay." Share the types of "okay" touches with your child: shake hands, pat on back, brief hug, high five, a kiss on the cheek. Make this a fun exercise by having your child act out the "okay" touches. Let your child know that "okay" touches are kind and respectful. "Okay" touches don't make us feel ashamed, scared, or unsafe. "Okay" touches can be done in public, and everyone can know about them.

4. Ask what kind of touch your child does *not* like. Listen to the answers. (There may be an "okay" touch your child does not like—such as tickling. Keep this in mind. Show respect to your child by not touching her in that way.) Then explain that "not okay" touches include hitting, kicking, scratching, pinching, or slapping. Point out how these kinds of touches are not respectful, and they make us feel unsafe.

5. Ask your child which parts of her body are private parts. Ask what the names are of the

opposite gender's private parts. Listen, then affirm or correct, your child's answers. Say, *"There are safety rules about touching or looking at private parts. Here are the rules about private parts that will help you know what is 'not okay' … "*

It is not okay for someone to touch your private parts.

It is not okay for someone to show you his or her own private parts.

It is not okay to touch someone else's private parts.

It is not okay for someone to ask you to touch his or her private parts.

It is not okay for someone to ask you to take your clothes off.

It is not okay for someone to take photos or videos of you with your clothes off.

It is not okay for someone to show you photos or videos of people without their clothes on.

(Some exceptions for health and hygiene purposes were covered in Chapter 5.)

6. Tell your child, *"All teenagers and adults know these rules. There are many good people in this world. Most people respect and obey the safety rules about private parts. But if someone ever*

breaks one of these rules, I want you to say, "No!" really loud, then get away from that person as soon as you can. I want you to come and tell me about it right away. I will help you. You will not be in any trouble for what happened. You will not be in trouble for telling me. I will not be mad at you. No matter what someone says to you, remember, I love you. You will never be in trouble for telling me if someone breaks a safety rule about private parts."

7. Tell your child: *"A person who does a 'not okay' touch might tell you to keep it a secret. But that would be a bad secret to keep. Just remember, once you are away from that person, I want you to tell me what happened. If anyone tells you that I won't believe you, or that I will be mad at you— that is not true. I will believe you. I will not be mad at you."*

8. Review some of the "not okay" rules by asking: *"What would you do if someone asked you to take off your clothes?"; "What would you do if someone showed you a picture of people with no clothes on?"; "What would you do if someone touched you on a private part?"* Let your child practice saying, "No!" and walking or running away in each scenario. Praise your child for her smart

reactions. Then ask: *"If someone told you not to tell about a 'not okay' touch that happened, would you still come and tell me about it?"* Listen to your child's response. If the question arises: *"What if that person says he's going to beat me up?"* assure your child that if she feels scared of the person, it is okay to agree to not tell—but only until she gets to a safe place. Once she finds you or another safe adult, she must tell what happened.

9. Review with your child which adults are safe to tell if you are not around. Highlight female role models, such as a grandmother, aunt, teacher, school nurse, trusted neighbor, or a police officer (male or female). Remind your child that the safety rules about private parts apply to *all* family members, and to *all* neighbors, friends, teachers, coaches, babysitters, and strangers. (A later chapter will deal with how to respond if your child discloses abuse.)

10. Let your child ask any questions she has. Listen carefully and give a thoughtful response. End your talk by telling your child how much you love her. Then do something fun together and move on to other subjects.

It becomes second nature for children to hear their parents instruct them with the "dos" and "don'ts" of life regarding their personal safety. Parents establish safety rules in many areas, such as: inside the house ("No throwing balls in the house"); outside ("Don't go in other people's houses without my permission"); traveling in vehicles ("Buckle your seat belt"); personal hygiene ("Wash your hands before eating"). Likewise, the discussion of "okay" and "not okay" touches can be a simple and direct conversation about their safety.

This conversation does not need to be long and drawn out, but simple, relaxed, and in straight-forward language. Do not tell your child stories of children being kidnapped, molested, raped, or killed by a child molester! Only give information that will educate and protect. There is no need to fill children with unnecessary fears. The tone of your conversation should be loving, confident, and informational … with no hysterics attached.

Here's an activity you can do with your child. To help your child understand that a boundary defines ownership, go outside and ask him to point out where your family's property stops and where the neighbor's property begins. Show him how a fence or other line goes all the way around your property. Share how everything inside the line belongs to your family. Everything outside the line belongs to someone else. (If in an apartment, you can use the dividing wall between units as the boundary.) Ask your child what things your family does to keep your house and yard nice (i.e. mow, rake leaves, water, take out trash, etc.) Point out that your family is responsible for taking care of your belongings and all that is on your property. The neighbor takes care of what belongs to the neighbor. Share how people should respect what belongs to someone else. A way your family shows respect to others is by not throwing your trash on someone else's lawn, and not taking things that belong to others without first asking their permission. Point out how we want others to respect what is ours, and we will respect what is theirs.

Let your child know that everyone has a special boundary for his or her own bodies. It's called skin. Ask your child to touch his skin. Tell your child: *"Your skin and all that is inside you is yours to take care of. No one should harm you or touch you in a way that is not okay."* (Review with your child the "not okay" behaviors under Point #5 above.) Let your child know: *"You have my permission to yell 'No!' at anyone who tries to break a safety rule about touching or looking at private parts."*

Our next chapter will address helping you and your child to set and hold acceptable boundaries involving the behaviors of others.

Personal Notes

7

It's Okay to Say "No" to an Older Person

"You're not the boss of me!"

It's funny to hear this familiar childhood anthem being robustly declared by a defiant little one. When uttered, a child is sending an unambiguous, verbal warning—a shot over the bow, in effect—letting someone know: "You don't have the right to tell me what to do!"

This is the kind of conviction children need to possess regarding their bodies, and how others touch them. Parents can begin to foster this sense of personal ownership by giving their children permission to say "No" or "No, thank you" to those who want to touch them in "okay" ways. This includes allowing children to refuse older, well-meaning family members who might only want a hug or a kiss. It's never too early to teach children to shake hands.

For decades, my family has known exactly when my Aunt Marguerite arrives at a family get-together. Most of us congregate in the family room or backyard, either because we're chatting, rooting for our favorite sports team, or enjoying the outdoors. No matter where we are, once one of the little ones runs through the house with a big, bright red lipstick imprint on the cheek, we know Aunt Marguerite has arrived! It has become part of our family lore. We call it "The Mark of Aunt Marguerite."

You might have a family member like my Aunt Marguerite. Exuberant. Affectionate. Expressive. There seems no escaping the hug, kiss, tickle, or rustling of hair. Although such a touch is well intentioned and innocent, a child might nonetheless feel uncomfortable being *subjected* to it. A tired or fussy child might pull away and say, "I don't want to!" or even respond with, "I don't like you!" Parents, embarrassed at such behavior, often respond by coaxing their child, "Oh, give Grandma a hug." Some parents up the pressure with an ultimatum, "If you don't give Grandpa a kiss, you won't get any dessert tonight." There's also the guilt response, "Uncle John is such a good uncle. He has been so nice to you, and you won't even give him a hug. Shame on you."

But what is happening here? Parents are coercing the child to perform. The message being sent to the child is, in essence: "Even if you don't want to be touched, you must do it anyhow, or I will be unhappy with you." This parental inference can prove confusing to a child who has been taught that her body is her own, and that no one is to touch her in a way that makes her feel uncomfortable.

So what is a parent to do?

Young children need examples that are consistent with the instructions they have been given. A child's desire to not be touched should be respected—even if that touch is done in an innocent context. Why? Because the child who is refusing to be touched in a particular way, or at that particular time, is setting a boundary with the other person—a boundary having to do with his or her *body*. This is something we want our children to feel confident in doing!

I was not always a respecter of children's personal space. As the adoring aunt of 25 wonderful nieces and nephews I can't wait to hug, kiss, hold, and snuggle them when I visit. Most the time they eat this affection up! But there are times that asking for a hug or kiss gets me a flat-out refusal. Years ago, I responded to such rebuffs by hugging and kissing them anyhow. I would impose myself on them, overpowering their objections. I did not realize it at the time, but that was very selfish of me. I was more concerned with meeting my need for affection than respecting the personal space of these little ones. To be perfectly honest, as an aunt, I had an entitlement attitude.

My perspective changed when I started investigating crimes against children. I saw how molesters had no regard for the personhood of children. Molesters wanted what they wanted … and nothing else mattered. The human dignity of children was not respected. Children were just a means to a sexual, self-gratifying end. Control, through manipulation or domination, was a repeated theme in the abuse. Child victims were told what to do and how to do it. Objections were often met with threats of retaliation. In their fear, guilt, and shame, or in a sense of hopelessness, children kept silent about the "secret."

When I listened to children's stories of abuse, the "aunt" in me wanted to scoop them up and hold them tight. I wanted to dry their tears and rock them in my arms in a gentle, protective hold. I wanted to calm their fears with an assurance that things were now going to get better. But I could not do any of those things. Why? Because their little bodies had been violated. The very last thing I wanted to do was assert myself into their personal space and physically touch them. Instead, during our time together I would ask their permission before doing something, or I'd give them options they could choose from.

"Thank you for coming to see me. Would you like to sit in this chair?" I'd say. If a child was small and needed help, I'd ask, *"Would you like me to help you up on the chair? Or do you want to do it yourself?"* When a child wanted to do it independently, I waited for the child to figure it out, or change his or her mind and ask me to help. *"Would it be okay if I put your coat over here while we talk?"* By letting the child determine how his or her body and possessions were to be handled, the child could experience a sense of control in the unfamiliar environment of the

interview room. The child could also see that what he or she said was important to me. This patient and courteous exchange optimized the chance for greater communication later when we would discuss what happened in the child's life.

As I contemplated my own interactions with my family, I realized I wanted my nieces and nephews to feel empowered to set boundaries with others also. The best way for me to do that was to model my acceptance and respect of their feelings. I began asking them if I could give them a hug. If they said, "no", I'd reply, *"That's okay. Maybe you will want to later."* Then I'd smile and change the subject. Even if they were being mean about it, I'd give the same response, sometimes adding, *"I love you."*

I am not suggesting that children should rule the home by their emotions. Obviously, a child who refuses to go to bed because she doesn't feel like sleeping needs to understand that there are certain rules that need to be obeyed. But wherever possible, give your child the option to make a choice and express her opinion. Then show respect for that choice. So often we just give children directions, "do this … do that." Greater confidence results when a child knows that what he or she says matters. And you will want them to have that confidence should they need to say "no" to a teen or adult who is touching them in the wrong way, or showing them something that is inappropriate.

Caution and sensitivity should be exercised when wanting your child to perform. With the arrival of Smartphones, Facebook, YouTube, FaceTime, Google+, and Skype the opportunities for your child to perform for others is at the tip of your fingers. Parental pride can overflow when a little one has learned a new song or mastered some ability. If your child really enjoys his moment in the sun, that's great! But if your child is uncooperative, please don't get upset, order, or shame the child into doing what you want. Wait for a better time, perhaps after a nap or after a meal, before asking your child to reenact his newest achievement.

You can train your child to express "no" in a polite way to any family member or friend whose physical contact is unwanted. Let your children know that if they don't feel like responding to someone's affection or playfulness, they can say, "No, thank you. I don't feel like hugging right now" or "No, thank you. I don't like to be tickled." If awkward moments occur or someone is offended, help the person understand how you are training your child. Say, *We are teaching Sarah to tell others when she doesn't want to be touched.* This puts others on notice that you and your child have open and honest conversations on the topic of uncomfortable or inappropriate touching. If someone has ill intentions toward your child, the person might now think twice about crossing those boundaries.

Demonstrating support for your child's boundary validates the prior instruction you gave—it is okay to say "no" to unwanted touch, even to an adult you know. Your support will help your child have greater confidence to refuse any "not okay" touches suggested by someone they know.

Teaching your child it is okay to say "no" to an older person also applies when your child gets that gut-level fear inside. Those "red flag" feelings need to be heeded. Let your child know that if he feels scared, confused, or upset by something that is happening, it is okay to say "no" to the person who is involved.

Let's consider babysitting situations.

Most children want to be "big" and independent. If your child is old enough to care for his own hygiene, he has no need for a babysitter's help. Your child might feel awkward if someone tries to touch him. He should know that it is okay to say to the babysitter, "No. I can do that by myself." This also applies to changing into a bathing suit, changing into pajamas, or taking a shower.

Applying medicine to private parts (for example, for a rash) should be done by your child if he or she is able; or by you before leaving your child with a babysitter. Instruct your child that if the babysitter tries to help with this, the child is to firmly say "No. If I need help I will ask my mom." Of course, it is very important for you to tell that directly to the sitter as well.

To help your child know when something is wrong, tell the babysitter what your rules are and say it in front of your child. Rules might involve TV viewing, computer usage, who is not allowed over, cell phone calls, etc. Let the babysitter know you have discussed all the "not okay" touches with your child and the rule about not having secrets. Ask the babysitter if she understands everything you have said. Later, without drilling your child with questions, casually ask you child how things went with the babysitter.

Another example: a neighbor friend suggests playing the game "Truth or Dare."

I am not a fan of this type of game because there is too much room for an older child to dominate a younger child. If your child has enjoyed playing it, then it will be helpful reviewing the following things the child can, and should, say "no" to:

- If a dare involves going into a hidden place with someone (like a closet or bedroom), it is okay to say "no" to the dare.

- If the dare is to eat or drink something, it is okay to say "no."

- If the dare has to do with kissing, it is okay to say "no."

- If any dare makes you feel uncomfortable, nervous, or embarrassed, it is important to pay attention to your feelings. It is okay to say "no."

- If the dare involves taking any clothes off, always say "no" because that is a "not okay" rule.

- If you say "no" to a dare and have a "yucky" feeling about the game, the game might not be safe. It's time to come home and talk about it with an adult.

A Code Word To Signal Trouble

Some families use a code word or phrase that only the parents and child know. If the child is away from home and is frightened or in need of help, he or she can call the parent and use the code word. The word or phrase should be unique enough to not be missed by the parent. It should not be a code that gives a warning to others who might be overhearing the child's conversation. The parent's response to the child's location should be immediate.

My brother, Tom, taught his twin daughters that no matter where they were, if something happened that made them feel uncomfortable, scared, or they knew was not right, he wanted them to call him right away. Tom made it clear: they were to call him any time—day or night—and just say, "Dad, come get us," and he would be on his way.

One weekend Tom's girls attended a sleepover with their 7th-grade girlfriends. It was a fun time until the host parents went upstairs to sleep. Around midnight, the girl whose home it was, decided to go into an online chatroom. My nieces had been taught the dangers of chatrooms. As their friends bantered back and forth with the online mystery man, the chatroom conversation turned sexual. My nieces got that sick feeling that warns of danger. They told their friends the conversation should end because the guy was a "creep" and "dangerous." But their concerns were immediately dismissed, even ridiculed, by their peers.

Tom's phone woke him out of the dead sleep. "Dad, come get us." Within 15 minutes Tom pulled up in front of the home. Both girls came out, carrying their overnight belongings. On the way home they explained what had happened. Tom could not have been prouder of his girls. They paid attention to that gut-level discomfort, recognized the unsafe situation, and made the right choice to keep themselves safe. The girls also saw how much their dad loved them. He proved good on his word to be there whenever they needed him, no questions asked.

All parents can instill a similar confidence in their children. It begins early with heart-to-heart parent-child conversations; the recognition of each person's value; the practices within the home that demonstrate respect; the teaching of proper boundaries; the training of how to handle difficult situations; and the ever-present, loving support of an approachable parent.

Children who have this kind of ongoing parental involvement in their lives will be less vulnerable to the dangers that might lurk nearby ... dangers that parents often do not see.

Password Protection

Parents can keep a password on their home computers and tablets so children or teens who come over can't log on without a parent knowing.

Personal Notes

8

Where Dangers Lurk

Wat kind of person molests a child?

Many people conclude that these perpetrators "must be sick" or "must be crazy." However, the vast majority of child molesters are neither sick nor crazy. No one forces them to offend. These molesters know their behaviors are morally wrong, illegal, and punishable. Yet they still choose to do it. Why? *Because it meets a selfish need.*

The terms "child molester" and "pedophile" seem interchangeable to most people. That's understandable, but there are differences. Simply put, a child molester is anyone who has sexual contact with a child, regardless of whether the child is willing or unwilling. A child molester can be a teen or an adult. A child molester can be male or female. Child molesters can be found in every race, religion, and social-economic group. They can work in any profession. Among the child molesters I have arrested have been babysitters, daycare workers, coaches, therapists, pastors, teachers, and even police officers.

Pedophiles are a specific category of child molesters. Pedophiles meet a certain psychological diagnostic criterion. To be diagnosed with pedophilia, the American Psychiatric Association in the *Diagnostic and Statistical Manual of Mental Disorders V* states a person must:

- be sexually aroused by, have intense, recurring sexual fantasies of, or be involved in sexual behavior with a prepubescent child or children (generally 13 years or younger);

- be aroused by, have sexual fantasies of, or be involved with a child for at least six months;

- be at least 16 years old, and

- be at least five years older than the child or children he or she is attracted to.

Pedophiles' sexual desires are *focused* on children and not on adults. Any pedophile who acts out his sexual desires becomes a child molester. Although categorized as a mental illness, pedophiles are not crazy. In fact, the contrary is true: they are shrewd and cunning.

Child molesters, who do not meet a pedophile profile, will molest children for a variety of other reasons. To get a better understanding of child molesters, let's briefly look at two categories developed by Dr. Park Dietz, a forensic psychiatrist. Dr. Dietz divided sex offenders into the two broad categories of *situational* and *preferential*. (Dietz, P. E. *Sex Offenses: Behavioral Aspects*. 1983)

Situational Child Molesters

Situational child molesters *do not prefer* children as sexual partners. They have sexual contact with children for a variety of reasons:

- boredom
- curiosity
- response to a stressful situation
- a lack of empathy or no moral boundaries
- substitution for a sexual partner
- low self-esteem or feeling socially inadequate
- anger
- the mere availability of the child.

Although situational child molesters tend to be impulsive, they do consider risks before offending. They are aware that their actions are wrong and criminal. Situational offenders generally have one or few victims.

When I speak to groups of parents or other caregivers there is generally a question about selecting babysitters. I always give this advice: *If at all possible, avoid having a teen boy babysit.* The statement generates a rumbling of responses: "You don't know the boy I use. He's great and my kids love him." "My son babysits and I trust him completely." "It really depends on who the boy is, doesn't it?" "My teen sitter comes from a good family."

I speak bluntly about the dangers of placing a hormone-induced teen boy in authority over small children. Disgusting as this might sound, there can be a temptation to experiment with sexual things when the teen sitter is bathing a child, sees a child unclothed, or changes a diaper. There is also the possibility of the teen using a child to stimulate himself by having the child sit on his lap, bounce up and down, play a game of "find what's in my pocket," or another sly trick.

Am I saying that all teen boys have an ulterior motive to sexually touch the children in their care? Absolutely not! Am I saying that it is unfair to place a teen boy in a position where he might be enticed by his own curiosity or lust to violate a child? Yes! It is just not worth the risk! It is not fair to the child who could become a victim. Nor is it fair to the teen, who, if he acts wrongly in this situation, could continue to molest. Despite what he is like on the outside, you have no idea if the boy you are having watch your child has been filling his head with pornographic images and only needs to have an *opportunity* to act out his curiosity or desire. Remember twelve-year-old Kenny? I believe it is a safer choice to have a reputable female babysitter care for your child than hiring a male.

Here is an example of a situational offender from one of my cases. The case will also serve as a good illustration of how a victimized child can be very reluctant to tell her secret.

Amber was eight years old and extremely tight-lipped. When I asked if she would agree to tell me the truth during our conversation, she said, "No." She made it clear: she did not want to discuss "what my dad did." Children who are reluctant to talk invariably have a deep-seated fear. It takes patience, and some exploring, to find out what type of fear is crippling a child's communication.

To approach the off-limit subject in the least threatening way, I told Amber she didn't need to tell me what her dad did "right now." I asked if, instead, could she tell me *where* she was when "whatever your dad did" happened. This brought her some immediate relief because it took the forbidden subject off the table. Amber could tell me where it happened but still keep her secret. It took many unobtrusive questions to gather enough small details from her to finally have an accurate picture of what was occurring at the time of the abuse—without actually discussing the abuse.

As Amber became more comfortable, I returned to the subject of what her father did. She said he wrestled with her in the tent when they were camping, but she did not like where he touched her. She eventually disclosed that her father had touched her vaginal area (over her clothes) on three separate occasions and locations: during the camping trip, in her bedroom, and on the living room couch.

I observed some troubling family dynamics the day I interviewed Amber and her mother. These gave me insight into the father's character and why Amber was so afraid to talk. During my interview with Amber, and later with her mother, Amber's father was repeatedly calling his wife's cell phone in an attempt to gain information about my investigation. The mother was flustered and visibly nervous each time her phone rang. Finally, I got on the phone with him. He explained to me that he was just checking on his wife's well-being. I told him she was fine, we were busy, and to stop calling. He said okay, but a few minutes later he called again, badgering his wife for more information. I spoke to him a second time and advised him not to interfere. I told him I would speak with him the next day and answer all his questions.

This guy was extremely controlling. He had no respect for others' boundaries. It was driving him nuts to not be the one steering this ship (the investigation). He was insistent on finding out what his wife and daughter reported. No wonder they were both afraid of him!

Getting into the mind of a child molester is something every detective must do to effectively engage the perpetrator in an interrogation. I use the term "engage" rather than "confront" because it better describes my approach. After hundreds of interviews with suspects, I can confidently say I have never hit a table, yelled, cursed at, or threatened a suspect. Unlike what movies and TV shows portray, detectives catch more flies with honey than with vinegar. I was highly successful at getting confessions because I assumed the persona of an "understanding friend" to the perpetrator.

When I interviewed Amber's father the next day, he flatly denied the allegations of sexual touching. So I assumed my "molester's best friend" persona. Soon he began to drop his guard. He shared how frustrated he was with his job, how lousy the financial markets were, how his wife was too busy working to have sex with him, how she spent more time with their daughter than him, and how taxing his daughter's behavior issues were getting. He emphasized how his daughter would suddenly "jump on him" when she wanted to play.

It was clear to me, this control freak's world was out of *his* control. Molesting his daughter was his way of asserting his dominance. It might have also served as a payback to his wife for her lack of sexual intimacy with him. This guy was a *situational* child molester. His real sexual interest was towards his wife, but he used his daughter as a substitute. He was angry. She was available. With a child, he could assert the dominance he was not experiencing in other areas of his life.

Now that his actions were known, his greatest need was to control his image as a good spouse and father, and thus dodge any suspicions of criminal behavior. It gave me the idea to emphasize to him how "stress can make a person do things they would not normally do." I cited how his wife's preoccupations with other matters left him alone and sexually frustrated; how the economy was brutal and unfair; how his daughter was overbearing by being so physically playful. Could it be, I suggested, that during his daughter's physical playfulness, he just had "a lapse in judgment" and touched her private parts? By emphasizing the "stress" aspect, I presented him with a seemingly *palatable excuse* for his behavior. With this scenario he could admit to the actual physical contact and claim it was a momentary "out of character" act. This way he could still maintain the facade of being a great dad and spouse.

I presented the excuse and he latched on to it. He admitted to touching her vaginal area (over her clothes), and even cited the same three incidents and locations that the child told me about. He thought the "stress" angle would exonerate him, but he was wrong. I started to discuss his motives—to strip away any illusion of "innocence." He eventually admitted to being aroused during these events. This confirmed his sexual motivation. These were not accidents, they were assaults. When I informed him that he was under arrest, he became indignant. He blamed his actions on eight-year-old Amber, "She came on to me! Each time! She came on to me! You tell the DA that!" Knowing how damning those words were, I replied, "Oh, I'll do better than that. I'll quote you in my report."

Let me make this very clear: no matter what kind of stress is in someone's life, no matter what the situation, nothing can excuse or justify sexually touching a child. Nothing.

Preferential Child Molesters

Dr. Dietz's second category of offender is the preferential child molester. These are the pedophiles discussed earlier. They *prefer* sex with children to sex with adults. They act upon their sexual fantasies of pre-pubescent children. A preferential child molester might prefer boys over girls, or vice-versa, or just prefer a child regardless of gender. They might prefer a certain age of child for a victim. These types of offenders victimize large numbers of children.

Pedophiles are so successful at offending because they are masters at not getting caught. They go to great lengths to deflect any possible suspicion. Preferential child molesters have learned to get away with their heinous crimes by shrewd cunning, careful planning, and a practiced exterior, all of which they use to camouflage their intention. Their ability to seduce children and to fool parents into trusting them is astounding!

Two children disclosed to me that their stepfather had sexually abused them for a long time. Later, when I interviewed their mother, I inquired about the nature of her and her husband's intimate relationship. I explained I was not trying to be intrusive, voyeuristic, or to embarrass her.

I told her when accusations are sexual in nature, it is helpful to understand the general nature of the parents' sexual relationship. It was important for me to consider any possible exposure the children might have had to sexual information.

This woman had a bewildered look on her face as she answered. When they were engaged, she explained, they had an active sexual relationship. It was "very normal," she thought. However, soon after their wedding he lost interest in having sex. Such a dramatic change was perplexing to her. It filled her with self-doubt, wondering why she was no longer desirable. It bothered her so much that she suggested they go to couples' therapy to help restore sexual intimacy. They went, but the therapy had not helped.

The answer to what puzzled her was now becoming very clear to me. Assuming the role of a healthy heterosexual adult served to divert any suspicions of his real motives. Her husband had courted and married her for one reason: to gain unlimited sexual access to her children. He was a pedophile … a preferential child molester.

These types of child molesters seek to establish credible reputations with adults. By actively participating in activities that cater to children, such reputations begin to build. It also endears them to both child and parent. The child-rich environment provides the pedophile with greater opportunity to select and seduce his victims.

It is easier for parents to trust someone that their child has already spent some enjoyable time with. An individual who relates in caring ways to children will likely be appreciated or admired by parents. A person's pleasant personality and good reputation can go a long way in winning over a parent's trust. Once there is a familiarity and comfort with a neighbor, family member, friend, teacher, coach, or group leader, vigilance can seem less necessary. However, it is these types of relationships where greater vigilance is needed.

Most Molestors Are Not Stangers

93% of child sex assault victims know their molesters.

(Douglas, Emily and D. Finkelhor,
Crimes Against Children Research Center, May 2005)

Those nearest to us are the ones who have the most access to our children. Just because a person shares our bloodline, faith, activities, or interests, does not mean the person shares our values and convictions. The derelict in the trench coat who hangs out in alleys should not be your biggest concern. Why? Because you aren't going to let your child hang out in an alley where an odd-looking stranger in a trench coat lurks! What you will do, however, is allow your child around people you know and trust, in places that you feel are safe.

Back when I was a new patrol officer, I interviewed my first child sexual assault victim. I met the 15-year-old girl and her mother at Social Services. (My agency didn't have a Crimes Against Children Unit at the time, nor was there a Child Advocacy Center available.) This young teen told me of her sexual abuse at the hands of her father. It had gone on for so long that she could not recall when it started. She described various sexual acts in an almost monotone voice. What I imagined as horrific experiences were being retold by this child as if they were common everyday things. I did not doubt she was telling the truth, but her lack of emotion puzzled me.

I carefully ventured a question that would prove to be incredibly revealing. *"Did you ever express to your father that you did not want to participate in the things he wanted you to do? If so, what was his response?"* This child, who'd sat there unflinching at the retelling of such horrors, suddenly burst into tears! "Yes! Yes! He pushed me away! He pushed me away!" she said, weeping and gasping, "He said he wouldn't love me anymore! He said he wouldn't love me anymore!"

As she sobbed uncontrollably, I got her some tissues and sat quietly. I finally understood the core of her heartbreak. This despicable father had manipulated her for years using rejection as his tool. She loved him and he knew it. He used her need for a father's love against her. He threatened to reject her and withhold his love if she did not comply with his sexual wishes. By the end of the interview all I could think of was getting this poor child away from this evil man.

Sometimes, the longer the period of abuse, the more deadened a child's affect becomes. The fear of loss can keep a child silent for years. Children who are victims of sexual abuse do not have a "typical" response. The responses can vary widely and for a myriad of reasons.

Hours later, I was in the Investigations Division when the father arrived to speak with detectives. I remember doing a double-take. This disgusting and vile individual stood there nicely dressed, mild-mannered, polite, looking as non-threatening as my own grandfather. I expected a guy in a trench coat; what I got was someone resembling Mr. Rogers. I went home that day disturbed at my own naivety. I remember saying out loud, "How am I going to know who the bad guys are?"

You have probably felt that way too, even while reading this book, and asked yourself: "How am I going to know who is safe for my child to be around?" Parents might not always know a book by its cover, but they can educate themselves about the behaviors that signal trouble.

Now that you know more about the types of child molesters, let's take a closer look at how they operate and how parents can counteract a molester's objectives.

Check Sex Offender Registries

Local and national sex offender registries can be accessed by the public. Find out who in the neighborhood might pose a threat to your child and warn your child to avoid that person and the person's house. Be aware: these registries do not list every offender. Some registries might not list juvenile offenders, or those who have misdemeanor sex convictions. Visit the National Sex Offender Registry: www.nsopw.gov or contact your local sheriff's office.

Do not think a person is safe just because his name is not on the registry.

Personal Notes

9

Grooming: Exploiting A Child's Vulnerability

Some children are quite verbal. Parents can wrongly assume that because their child is verbal, they will always know what's happening in their child's mind and life. That might be true most of the time, but when it comes to being sexually touched, even the most verbal child might clam up.

Most parents believe they can interpret their children's moods and know if something is bothering them. Parents in some of my cases have told me they were sure nothing happened to their child because "I would have seen something" or "my child would have told me."

When it comes to sexual molestation, many child victims neither tell nor exhibit the types of responses we might think would be "normal." Instead of screaming, a child might freeze from fear. Rather than seek help, a child might not disclose the victimization because of threats. A child might choose not to disclose abuse because the offender is bribing with gifts. The type of relationship a child has with the offender factors heavily into whether the child tells. If the offender is someone the child loves, the child might not want that person to get into trouble or go to jail. An offender can convince a victim that *both of them* will be in trouble if the child's parent finds out what *they* have been doing. This manipulative wording by the offender paints the child as a willing partner, and therefore deserving of the parents' wrath.

Molesters, particularly pedophiles, groom their child victims in order to maximize their chance for success. Grooming means to prepare or train for a particular purpose or activity. Other words that describe this action are: prepare, prime, ready, condition, tailor, coach, train, instruct, drill, teach, and school. It's a frightening and sickening thing to think of another person systematically seducing a child for sex, but that is what grooming does.

I was training a new detective in the Crimes Against Children Unit when the mother of a 13-year-old boy called to complain that an adult friend, Ben, had behaved inappropriately towards her son, David. They had known Ben for two years. Ben was an intelligent and seemingly kind retiree. Ben was physically fit, loved sports, and had a stellar reputation as a volunteer rescue worker in the community. Ben and David often spent time together through a mentoring program. Recently, David had become increasingly uncomfortable when alone with Ben. David finally confided to his mother that Ben had placed his hand on David's thigh and rubbed it while driving David home from a sports event. This made David very uncomfortable.

We interviewed David and determined that no criminal act had taken place. However, there were many indicators Ben might be a child molester, grooming David as a future victim. We ran Ben's background and found that 10 years earlier he had been convicted of sexually molesting two boys, both about 12 years of age. Ben served his prison time and completed three years of court ordered sex offender therapy. Ben was under no restrictions regarding contact with minors. Ben's crime occurred when there was no sex offender registry, so his crime remained unknown to the public. In the meantime, Ben began volunteering with a non-profit organization to mentor young boys. David's mother was divorced and the idea of a man investing time with her son was very appealing.

Ben voluntarily came in to talk with us. When we told him the matter involved his relationship with David, and that we knew of his prior convictions, Ben was surprisingly open. "I'm a pedophile," he said. We inquired about his interactions with David. Ben's story of what occurred in the car matched David's account. Ben's actions were very odd and inappropriate, but Ben knew he had not crossed the criminal line.

All of us knew he was heading towards it.

Ben was relaxed and open, so I decided to make the most of our time by asking questions about his sexual interest in children. I asked how he groomed boys, what type of boy he was attracted to, and how he gained the trust of boys and their parents. Ben's answers provided an inside look at how pedophiles work.

Our conversation was recorded with his knowledge. (I used it later as a teaching tool in my academy course, and for training new detectives in our Crimes Against Children Unit. After all, it isn't every day that a person will admit he is a pedophile.)

Grooming

Child molesters often groom children before they make a sexual advance.

"Grooming" means "to prepare or train someone for a particular purpose or activity."*

Other words that describe this action are: "prepare, prime, ready, condition, tailor, coach, train, instruct, drill, teach, and school." **

*New Oxford American Dictionary
** Oxford American Writers Thesaurus

As one who cares for a young child, you will find the following excerpts from my interview with Ben disturbing, but enlightening. Ben's view of himself, his victims, and his crimes reflect classic pedophile attitudes and behaviors.

Ben's grooming techniques demonstrate how significant parental involvement is in reducing children's vulnerability to molesters.

What did you do as part of your grooming pattern?

Ben: *Do all kinds of activities with the kid. Take him everywhere. The kid I was convicted of molesting, I knew for about three years before I made any advances towards him ... of course, he had a stepfather who was pretty bad, and his real father he never knew.*

Child molesters, particularly pedophiles, recognize the inherent need children have for parental attention and approval. This relational need is met primarily through spending time together and having conversation. Ben was willing to take this boy "everywhere" in order to build a rapport with him. Being together gave Ben and the boy opportunity to talk, laugh, and learn about each other. These interactions built connection and trust between them.

Lack of a father's attention and involvement in a child's life contributes to a child's vulnerability. Ben was keenly aware of this. Filling this emotional gap in the boy's life made Ben more valuable and more needed by the boy. It also endeared Ben to the boy's mother. Ben was patient, biding his time while schmoozing the boy and his mother. He waited until he felt a bond had been made and he was safe enough to make his first sexual advance.

Victims are less likely to tell about sexual contact if it means they might lose a relationship that meets a deep personal need. Children who love their offender might choose to keep silent—even forgive the offender—rather than face an uncertain future not having that person in their life.

Your child needs an involved and caring father—or father figure—in his or her life. I realize that not all children have a father in the home, and that many wonderful single mothers do incredible jobs raising fine children. But the truth is, children without involved fathers have a vulnerability that molesters look to exploit. If you are a dad, be involved, and be your child's hero! If you are a single mom, don't let just any man into your child's life; look for a person of proven character with whom your child can spend time in group settings.

How did you gain the trust of these boys?

Ben: *You gain trust by doing a lot of things together and keeping your word. If you say you're going to do something, you do it! Another thing is to convince them that you're not going to talk about anything, that whatever you talk about is just between the two of you. I'll keep his secrets. I'm not out there to spy on him or go run to his folks to tell them about what we talk about. I think kids are looking for that a lot.*

Ben knew that consistency, dependability, and follow-through by an adult help a child feel loved and more trusting. We all know stories of children emotionally wounded by a dad or mom who didn't keep his or her word, or who failed to follow through on a promise. Ben made sure he never disappointed his intended victim. His devoted attention had a malevolent purpose. By convincing his victims they could trust him with their deep dark secrets, Ben opened the door to having something to blackmail them with. Ben would be a boy's buddy, a confidant, and never breathe a word to the boy's parents about anything wrong the boy was doing (in David's case it was smoking pot). Keeping secrets is a common grooming technique. Once Ben knew the things that could get a boy in trouble, he had ammunition to keep the boy quiet should the child threaten to expose Ben's sexual advances.

What Molestors Look For In A Victim

- Emotional neediness
- Isolation
- Low self-esteem
- Limited parental involvement
- Accessibility

Your consistent love and dependability will plant you as the solid rock in your child's life. Some of the most precious moments you can spend with your children is when they go to bed at night. When you tuck them in, ask how they are, and talk over the events of the day, or pray with them; it opens opportunities to know what is happening in their little hearts and minds. Let them freely share their world, their thoughts, their fears, and their silliness with you. Show your child that whatever he or she entrusts to you is safe, and will never be used to humiliate or coerce them. These little nighttime chats nurture contentment and imprint precious memories that say "mom and dad will be there for me to talk to."

How did the topic of sex come up with David?

Ben: *He wanted to know how to get a girlfriend—that's not really sex, I guess—and maybe get a little sexually involved with her. I told him he was a little too young for that. I talked with him about whether he had any friends that he played around sexually with. He said, 'no.' Uh ... he really kind of felt uncomfortable talking about sex at all.*

During their time together, Ben and David talked about many things. As a young boy approaching puberty, David became interested in having a girlfriend. Ben made the most of this topic. Notice how Ben turned the conversation with David towards sexual acts? Portraying himself as someone looking out for David's best interests, Ben discourages David from any sexual contact with girls, citing how David was "too young" for such activity. Yet Ben had no hesitance introducing the idea of David experimenting sexually with *male* friends. Ben's suggestion implied that this was an acceptable alternative for David to consider. Ben tried to enhance David's sexual curiosity and he did so with the clear intention of capitalizing on it. Ben would be more than happy to tutor David and "help" him navigate this new world of sex. Ben had used this modus operandi before. Fortunately for David, he was so uncomfortable with the topic of sex that Ben did not press the matter. Paying attention to his uncomfortable feelings prompted David to talk with his mother and it kept him from becoming a victim.

What type of child are you attracted to?

Ben: *We are really good at being able to groom a kid. For a lot of pedophiles, and people who abuse kids, it's a one or two time thing with a kid, and that's it. But for me, it is a long process of grooming. It's probably the physique of a kid, I mean, if they're smaller and more vulnerable ... I have an attraction to young males. I shouldn't have gotten into a friendship with them. My motives were pure at the time, for sure. It can be very beneficial to a young guy to have a relationship, especially if they don't have the best relationship with their folks.*

It is interesting how Ben separates the two groups: there are "pedophiles" and "people who abuse kids" … as if pedophiles do not abuse kids. This is typical pedophile thinking. A pedophile will say he "loves" children, not that he "abuses" children. Ben separates himself from those who quickly molest and move on. Ben seems uncomfortable with the word *molest* so he refers to those who have "a one or two time *thing* with a kid." Ben prides himself on the fact that he likes to groom a child for a long time.

The children Ben wants to seduce have a certain look—prepubescent males, small, vulnerable. Ben admits he should have avoided getting into a "friendship" with the boys, but then quickly justifies the relationship as having great value for the child. Ben believes the boys he grooms are "benefiting" from his "pure motives." He contends he is providing what is lacking in their home life and parental relationships … sadly, he is probably right. However, Ben has an agenda, and desires that are anything but pure.

How does the relationship progress?

Ben: *The excitement comes for me, and I don't get actually sexually excited, but it's what I call 'the chase'—to seduce him, that's what I enjoy. One kid, he started talking about sex non-stop one day, so I just asked him if I could get him sexually excited. I wanted … offered … to feel him up and give him an erection. But it doesn't mean to masturbate him. The kid that I was convicted for—that kid let me masturbate him.*

Confused? So were we. Ben explained *his* thinking. Ben believed fondling a young boy to the point of sexual arousal wasn't masturbating him; masturbation only happens if the boy ejaculates. For Ben, that was a big difference. Where the law of sexual assault on a child is concerned, there is no difference!

Ben makes a Freudian slip too; he says, "I wanted," but quickly amends the word to "offered." "Wanted" revealed his actual motive. The word "offered" made him appear more innocent and altruistic, as if he were doing the boy a favor. And despite his years of therapy, Ben still placed blame for his crime on his victim: he "*let me* masturbate him." Ben said his excitement came from "the chase," the seduction of the child. Remember, pedophiles fantasize about victimizing children. So the long grooming process no doubt *did* sexually excite Ben.

Beyond satisfying emotional and relational needs of a child, a molester might give gifts as part of the grooming process. Imagine a child craving to have the newest video game or go to a professional sports event. The offender starts providing things that normally are completely out of the child's reach. The relationship becomes an increasingly valuable friendship because of what the child is gaining materially. But the gifts are really bribes. The offender might eventually promise a gift in exchange for a sexual act, or give a gift to reward compliance, or hold out the promise of a major gift in the future to insure the child's silence. A victim once told me that his abuser promised to buy him a sports car when he turned 16—but only if the boy did not tell.

Red Flags: Intrusive Touches

- Massages
- Tickling
- Passionate kisses
- Sleeping in the same bed
- Blowing "raspberries" on child's stomach
- Back rubs
- Stroking of hair
- Wrestling / rough housing
- Cuddling or "spooning"
- Holding hand or rubbing leg while driving

Defense lawyers come up with all kinds of explanations for their child-molesting client's actions. One attorney argued that the defendant was merely engaged in "sex education" when he fondled the child. Another argued the defendant was checking the child for "sexual diseases." Another lawyer said his client was only seeing if the child was developing correctly. Any reasonable juror would be able to see through these smoke screens. At least we hope they could.

Former Penn State University Football Coach Jerry Sandusky is a poster-boy for pedophiles. He was a respected member of the community. He even started a program for at-risk youth. This gave him access to boys who came from lower income, troubled homes; and many boys who were in need of a father figure. Jerry soon began violating boundaries with boys he spent individual time with.

Listen to how Sandusky responds to filmmaker John Ziegler's inquiry about allegations that Sandusky had sexually abused young boys:

Sandusky: *Because I didn't. Yeah, I hugged them. Maybe I tested boundaries. Maybe I shouldn't have showered with them. Yeah, I tickled them. I looked at them as being probably younger than even some of them were. But I didn't do any of these horrible acts and abuse these young people. I didn't violate them. I didn't harm them.*

Ziegler: When you say maybe you tested boundaries, why would you be testing boundaries?

Sandusky: *Why would I be testing boundaries? I may have tested boundaries because of my enthusiasm and my yearning to make a difference in lives. Because of my efforts to make a difference in their lives.*

Sandusky considers himself a good man who cares deeply for troubled kids. He writes off his boundary breaking behaviors by saying only that he "maybe" should not have done them. He steadfastly contends, "I didn't harm them."

Society is slowly realizing that boys experience the same psychological and emotional damage as girls when victimized by sexual abuse. Sandusky did, in fact, cause great harm to his victims.

Think About It

Two men were eye-witnesses to Jerry Sandusky sexually abusing a boy. Neither intervened nor reported it to police. Both men were afraid of losing their jobs by speaking out against a popular and successful coach. What would you have done?

Back to my interview with Ben …

Ben told me he was attracted to young males who have small physiques and were more vulnerable. I have known other pedophiles with sexual interest in prepubescent children. Later in our conversation, Ben seemed pleased with himself when he told me that he had groomed "a couple kids" but never made sexual advances towards them. Ben said, "I grew out of it with them." Ben took credit for not acting on his attraction to these boys. A far more likely explanation is that while Ben was grooming them, the boys grew up, and developed physically to the point where they were no longer desirable to Ben.

Molesters can use many non-abusive "okay" touches to be part of their interaction with a child. A hug, pat on the back, possibly hand holding, wrestling, and tickling will get the child accustomed to the molester's physical touch. All appears normal, benign, and caring. However, the "okay" touch is just the warm-up before the pitch. "Okay" touches, like back rubs, are the precursor to intrusive touches. Parents should have a red flag go up if anyone is giving their child a massage. Most child molesters will try to "test the water" slowly; they move from "okay" touches into the intrusive touches, and watch to see how the child reacts. If a child reacts negatively and overtly, the molester might quickly pull away and go no further, out of fear of being discovered.

An offender who has an established non-sexual relationship with a child presents a very real threat. The established rapport between them enhances the child's confusion when the offender starts to test the child's boundaries. The targeted child might interpret the offender's touch as being "okay" because of *who* is doing the touching. The perpetrator depends on the respect, love, or authority he has developed with the child to create confusion within the child's mind and emotions. The child believes this person cares, yet cannot reconcile why the person is doing these "not okay" things. Such a fog might cause the child to be more reluctant to oppose the person's advances, particularly when the offender is making assurances that what is happening is "okay." Boundaries crossed by a trusted person can cause a young child to second-guess the gut feelings that warn of danger.

Be Cautious Of Someone Who ...

- Makes sexual jokes around a child.
- Bullies a child.
- Play games involving disrobing.
- Engages in depantsing a child.
- Asks a child to keep secrets.
- Approves of a child breaking rules.
- Communicates secretly or excessively with a child.
- Is more interested in being with children than adults.
- Seems overly interested in a child.
- Offers to babysit or take a child overnight to give the parents a break.
- Does activities with children when parents are not invited or involved.

It bears repeating: should your child be reluctant to go somewhere or be with someone, take the time to ask why.

Ask how he or she feels about a person or place; and be careful not to immediately dismiss the child's hesitance or perceptions as being "silly" or "ridiculous." Even if it makes no sense to you, do not place a child in a situation where he or she feels fearful. Those gut-level feelings—in parent or child—are important to heed!

In some cases, molesters will introduce pornography as a tool in their seduction and abuse of a child. The pornographic images shock a child, making the child feel more intimidated and controlled. The perpetrator can use the images to instruct the child on how to satisfy the offender's lust. The continued exposure and pressure breaks down the child's resistance to participating in sexual acts.

Let's take a moment to consider some red flags. When someone offers to spend one-on-one time with your child; wants to take your child overnight; or frequently gives your child gifts—or gives *expensive* gifts—it is time for you to pay attention. Other danger signals include any adult or teen who likes to spend time with younger children, does not have a group of same age friends to socialize with, uses the current youth jargon in conversations, or inserts himself into childish relational gossip. Limit your child's exposure to this person and do not let them spend time together alone. Be wise, pay attention to your gut, and take precautions. Be careful not to brand the person as a "child molester" to family, friends, or organizations without having proof. Parents need to be cautious—not alarmists!

Not all molesters groom their victims. Children can be victimized with no advance warning. This is why children need to clearly understand boundaries for their body and know how to seek help if those boundaries are crossed. Wise parents will remain watchful of grooming patterns and not hesitate to make adjustments in how they allow others to relate to their children should they become uncomfortable. Parents should always listen to their gut feelings.

In either situation, one thing is certain, an offender who has made his move wants to keep it a secret from you! The next "must have" parental conversation with children will address the issue of secrets.

Personal Notes

10

Understanding Good vs. Bad Secrets

Molesters know the key to successfully getting away with violating your child's body is the subversion of your child's allegiance to authority figures, particularly you. Whether it is through grooming by a pedophile, or by threats or intimidation from a child molester: the offender seeks to be the number-one influence, the ultimate voice, in your child's mind and heart. Once the line has been crossed, and a "not okay" action has been committed, the perpetrator's voice of authority has one resounding message to your child: DO NOT TELL! Discovery is the molester's worst fear, so making your child keep the secret is paramount.

An essential conversation to have with your child involves "good" vs. "bad" secrets. Once an offender takes the risk of exposing a child to sexual information (pornography or the taking of naked videos/photographs), bodily exposure (the child's or the molester's nudity), or sexual contact (of the child's or the molester's body), the child faces a terrible dilemma: "Do I tell?"

Offenders can use guilt to manipulate victims into silence. Offenders place blame on their victims by accusing the child of not objecting to, or not stopping, what the offender was doing. A molester might tell a child how much they "both liked" what took place. The offender might tell the child that he could not help himself because the child was "so pretty." A child might feel at fault for the assault thinking the abuse happened because he or she somehow misbehaved. An offender is likely to tell the victim, "If you say anything *we* will get in trouble." Guilt can silence a child who does not want to get into "more trouble" by telling.

Fear also can be used in a variety of ways to intimidate a young victim into silence. A man I arrested told his two stepdaughters that if they didn't perform the sex act he wanted they would go back to living in a car with their mother. One of the girls, who was reluctant to speak of her abuse, told me, "I don't want to lose our new car." It seemed like an odd response until I realized that this man had a really decked-out SUV, a very cool car to a child her age. It was so much nicer than the old beat-up car they were living in before this man befriended and married their mother. The girls were terrified at the thought of returning to a homeless lifestyle. The offender made it clear to them that if they objected to sexual acts, or ever told anyone, they would lose the comfort of sleeping in a warm bed with a roof over their heads.

Family-Type Risk Factors

Family structure is the most important risk factor in child sexual abuse. Children who live with two married biological parents are at low risk for abuse. The risk increases when children live with stepparents or a single parent. Children living without either parent (foster children) are 10 times more likely to be sexually abused than children that live with both biological parents. Children who live with a single parent who has a live-in partner are at the highest risk: they are 20 times more likely to be victims of child sexual abuse than children living with both biological parents.

(Fourth National Incidence Study of Childhood Abuse and Neglect, Report to Congress; Sedlack, et. al., 2010)

In another case, a live-in boyfriend introduced sexual acts to his girlfriend's daughter by exposing her to pornography. He told her, "All families do this." He convinced this child that her mother already knew what was happening between them. He told the child that since it was "a family secret" if she ever did talk to her mother about it her mother would slap her hard in the face. In this child's mind, she would face the wrath of her mother, as well as the offender, if she told anyone. Of course, this was all a lie, but she didn't know it. It left the little girl feeling she had nowhere to turn. Fear of punishment, fear of rejection, fear of disapproval, fear of not being believed—all factored into the emotional blackmail.

We previously have discussed how gifts or bribes can win silence from a victim. The offender might gain a child's approval and loyalty by providing the child with otherwise unattainable items. One offender I interviewed knew that his victim loved basketball, so he took the boy to professional NBA basketball games. The boy really didn't want that to end! Another offender let his victim drink alcohol. He gave parties for the boy and the boy's friends.

Remember, child sexual abuse comes in many forms. Sexual abuse might not always involve touching. Sometimes it is in the form of sexual exploitation (exposure of child's intimate parts via cell phones, cameras, webcams, etc.) A child might be uncomfortable with taking his clothes off for a picture, but could be persuaded to do it for a brand-new toy. "It will be our secret," says the offender.

Most adults will tell a parent if they have bought something for a child. There is usually a story that goes with it. The details are readily offered even before the parent asks. But parents who see their child in possession of new unexplained items or money should have a conversation with their child. Inquire along these lines: *Where did you get that? Who gave it to you? Did you have to do anything to get it?* If your child's answer makes sense, and is delivered in a stress-free way, there might be nothing to be concerned about.

However, if you see that your child stumbles over his answer, or show signs of embarrassment or fear, something might be wrong. Don't panic and assume your child is being groomed for or has been the victim of sexual abuse. It could be that your child took it from a friend's house, or stole it from a store, or took the money out of your purse/wallet. Let your child explain and follow-up as needed.

The discussion with your child about "good" vs. "bad" secrets can go something like this:

"When somebody has a birthday, it's fun to pick out a special present for that person and wrap it up. We wrap the present so that the birthday person doesn't know what we bought. It is our secret. A secret is when we know something that nobody else knows.

"There are good secrets and there are bad secrets. It is very important for you to know the difference. Good secrets make us and other people happy. Good secrets are only kept for a very short time, and then everyone knows what the secret is—like when a present is opened!

"Bad secrets make us feel sad, or hurt, or scared. Bad secrets make us feel yucky inside and we start to worry. If you see a person do something wrong, that person might tell you, 'Don't tell anyone! It's our secret.' Remember, that is a bad secret. If a person makes you do something you did

not want to do, then says to you, 'Don't tell!'—then that is a bad secret.

"I love you so much. If someone wants you to keep a bad secret its very important for you to tell me about it right away. I want to know if anything ever happens that makes you feel nervous, embarrassed, sad, scared, or hurt. I can help you when you talk to me. Remember, I will never be angry with you for what happened.

"Even if the person says he will do something mean to you if you tell the bad secret, don't worry, I will make sure that doesn't happen. Come and tell me right away. I will believe you, and I will take care of you."

Ask your child if everything you said was clear and if there are any questions. Review with your child the people who are safe to tell, should the child know a bad secret. Always conclude your talk with a hug and a verbal affirmation of love. Children should be assured after such a conversation of how special they are and how proud you are of them.

Activity: Is It A Good Or Bad Secret?

Ask your child to identify the following secrets as good or bad. Ask your child how he would feel in this situation and what he would do. Listen until your child has shared all his thoughts. If he reaches the wrong conclusion help him understand the right answer.

- A friend at school says his dad hits him and he is afraid. He tells you not to tell.

- Tonight the whole family is going out for a special treat. Your mom says to keep it a secret.

- A person you know shows you pictures of people with no clothes on. He tells you not to tell.

- A babysitter has friends over when she is not supposed to. She gives you extra desert and tells you to keep it a secret from your parents.

- Your brother is getting a new basketball for his birthday. It is wrapped up in the closet. Dad says not to tell your brother before the birthday party.

- Someone shows you his private part. He tells you not to tell.

- You see a friend take something from a store without paying. The friend tells you not to tell.

- A girl at school tells you she made a special card for the teacher. She asks you to keep it a secret.

- Someone you know touches your private parts. He tells you not to tell or he will be really mad at you.

- During a game someone dares you to take off your pants. You say, "No!" What should you do now?

Personal Notes

11

Building Trust: Your Pre-emptive Strike Against Molesters

In times of fear, confusion, or sadness, will *you* be the person your child runs to? I believe you can be. But it will not be automatic. It will not happen if there is no trust. Will *your* wisdom be what echoes in your child's heart, and guides him or her to a safe place when he or she is under pressure? I believe it can be. But not without trust. *Will your child talk to you?* Yes, if you build trust.

This book is about laying a protective foundation in your child's life. There are many, many factors that apply, but the key to making this foundation firm is trust. Just as you nurture love and security, you must nurture trust. Trust is the firm belief in the reliability, truth, ability, or strength of someone. Here are my suggestions on how to help trust grow.

Detective Diane's 10 Ways to Build Trust with Your Child

1. Spend *time* with your child. Appreciate what is unique about your child.

Take time to be with your child. Do interactive things that your child will enjoy. A happy and engaged child will be more open to talking. Try not to compare your child to other children. Instead find things to compliment and praise about your child's abilities, character, and personality. Remember, harsh words wound deeply. If a child is called "stupid" or someone who "can't do anything right," or is labeled "the stubborn one"—trust will be very hard to build. Rather, let affirming words draw your child closer to you.

2. Practice *patience* when listening.

It is very easy to dismiss children. We can finish their sentences for them; tell them to go away; half-heartedly listen while focused elsewhere; or point them to someone else. We don't realize that to cut a child short is to cut that child off. What is important to children can be totally boring and seemingly irrelevant to us. Building trust with children means valuing them and their little worlds.

As much as possible, when your child is talking: stop, make eye contact, and listen patiently. Your active listening will make a big deposit in the trust-bank. Your child will feel loved, knowing you cared about what was shared, and about how he or she felt. Should something troubling happen—regarding emotional red flags or inappropriate touch—your child will be far more open to sharing it with you.

3. Share your family's *values*.

What kind of character do you want your child to have? Begin shaping it by sharing what you value, and then model those values. When your child demonstrates character traits such as honesty, unselfishness, or kindness, express how proud this makes you feel. If your child does something wrong, look at it as an opportunity to discuss decision-making, consequences, and choices. Your child needs to have values, ideals, and a sense of purpose to guide his or her life. Always talk to your child in an age-appropriate way so he or she will understand your message about what is important. And remember, never withdraw your love because of a child's mistake or bad behavior.

4. Always tell the *truth*.

There are times when sharing details with your child should be limited, but always seek to give an answer that is honest. If a pet has died, say so, yet use sensitivity about sharing details of the death. If the application of medicine to your child's injury will sting, let him or her know that fact, instead of saying, "This won't hurt." Your child needs to feel secure that if he or she has questions, you are sure to have the reliable answer.

5. *Keep* your word.

Make realistic promises to your child and do your very best to keep them. Many children have felt devastated by parents who don't keep their word. Trust comes through the assurance that what you say is what you will do. Children need to know you will be there for them.

If circumstances make a promise impossible to keep, take a moment to explain why to your child and do so in a caring way that acknowledges your child's disappointment. Your child will be less likely to internalize the situation as a personal rejection.

6. Apply *discipline* with fairness and restraint.

A parent's response to a child's disobedience should be measured and controlled, not volatile and unpredictable. Be sure your rules are clear and understandable to your child. He or she should know that if rules are broken, there will be consequences. Try to avoid any appearance of favoring one child over another. When discipline is applied fairly and consistently, your child will grasp that you mean what you say. Follow-through, even with discipline, serves to make your child feel secure.

7. *Admit* when you are wrong.

If you make an error, admit that to your child. And don't be too proud to ask a child's forgiveness when you blow it. Parents who can acknowledge losing their tempers, saying something they shouldn't have said, or failing to keep a promise, demonstrate how important it is to talk about problems, mistakes, and uncomfortable feelings. Trust is built when your child sees that you are willing to acknowledge your imperfection. You demonstrate to your child that such discussions do not have to be a fearful thing.

8. *Respond*, rather than overreact.

Children need to know that making a mistake is not the end of the world. At home or in public children will make mistakes, or not perform to a parent's expectations, or do something they have no control over (i.e. wetting the bed.) A parent who overreacts by berating or insulting the child will drive a wedge of alienation between them. If the result of a confrontation is that your child is humiliated, you have handled the matter incorrectly. Children will not trust someone who shames them. When you are frustrated—and at times all parents will be—take a deep breath, walk away to compose yourself, and then address what needs to be addressed without making a personal attack on your child.

9. *Compassion* encourages communication.

Small children experience their own types of stressful situations that produce uncomfortable feelings. It could be a sense of rejection when a friend doesn't want to play with them; insecurity at being chosen last when teams are picked; humiliation at being called a name; fear of being pushed around or threatened on the playground. Taking the time to inquire about their feelings, listen to their hurts, and offer encouraging and affirming responses will enhance their sense of security. They will know you care about what's bothering them, and that you will be there when they are hurting.

10. *Walk* your talk.

Children are not little adults, as some say. They are children. And all children are impressionable. Parents can influence their child's character development with the consistent modeling of noble attributes, such as honesty, respect, love, fairness, wisdom, patience, confidence, strength, and self-control. Practicing what you preach shows you are the real deal, steady and reliable, a person to seek out in time of need.

You are not a bad parent if you miss one of these aims, or apply them variably. The point is to remember them, and keep them in your mind as goals. You can see from all we've talked about in this book, it is so important for you to have specific conversations with your child to help build a trusting relationship, promote personal safety, and prevent sexual abuse. One-on-one time with you helps your child learn that his or her body is special, with each part having a specific name and job to do. Your child learns that private parts must be respected and cared for properly. These lessons become solidified when your child observes you modeling that respect by what you say and do, and in what you allow or disallow within your home. Safety rules establish boundaries that help your child understand what is "okay" and "not okay" regarding how bodies are touched or viewed. When you give permission to your child to reject touches that make him or her feel uncomfortable—even from family or friends—your child's confidence grows. Conversations with you will teach your child how to pay attention to the inner feelings that warn of danger, and know how to react if danger comes.

Through all these things, you are spending time with your child, reaffirming your love, your availability, your approachability, your willingness to listen, believe, and respond protectively to any situation in your child's world.

Here are a few suggestions on how to increase your approachability.

- Help your child work through problems and experience success. It's good for children to face reasonable challenges, whether its a puzzle, homework, sports, or completing a chore. Help your child succeed by giving clear instructions and regular encouragement. Praise your child's progress and accomplishments! Everyone needs a cheerleader in his or her corner.

- Have a sense of humor. Enter the fun worlds of tea parties or superheroes with young children. Perhaps read a funny book to your child, one chapter each night. Joke about the silly things that happen during the day, even innocent mistakes. Grumpy or critical parents are not easy to approach; but joy and laughter are great bonding agents.

- Give your child one-on-one time. That is a big bill for a busy parent to fill. But the moments just between the two of you will leave an indelible mark on your child's heart. Running errands together, taking a walk, playing a game, or prayers at bedtime, all allow for sweet exchanges of conversation. This reinforces the message: Being with you and knowing what you think and feel are important to me.

- Remain calm when things go bad. Few things are more frightening to a child than a parent who is out of control. Try to keep a proper perspective about the small things. A broken dish, a lost toy, a ruined outfit, a messy room … do not merit an outburst of anger. If you can take a deep breath and calmly focus on the matter at hand, your child will see that you are the go-to person when life becomes frustrating or unexpected things happen.

Personal Notes

12

If Your Child Discloses Sexual Abuse

Parents who apply the principles in this book will be investing not only in their child's protection but also in fostering a deeper, trusting relationship concerning all of life for the future. Sadly, however, despite all the care and caution parents provide, there is no 100 percent guarantee that a child will never be approached by a molester. I wish there were.

Disclosures of sexual abuse can come in direct or indirect ways. A child might say something indirect, like "My grandpa likes to sleep in my bed," or "I don't like going to my uncle's house," or "Johnny is mean sometimes." These statements give no details of abuse, but they should prompt an appropriate inquiry by a parent to clarify what the child is really saying. Appropriate questions are non-leading, non-accusatory questions.

Indications of sexual abuse can include children who display sexual behavior, like "humping" something, or using sexual terms they are too young to know or understand. Older children might inquire about whether they could get pregnant at their age, or disguise the disclosure by talking about "a friend who is being abused." Again, good follow-up questions should be asked.

A little girl told her teacher, "My brother sexed me." The teacher appropriately reported possible abuse to authorities. When I interviewed the girl she told me the same thing. Through non-suggestive questioning I learned that "sexed" to her meant to be kissed. Her brother gave her a kiss and she thought that was sex. There was no sexual abuse.

Direct disclosure might be prompted when a child realizes the sexual acts or indecent exposures she has been exposed to are not "normal" behaviors. A child might disclose after seeing a safety presentation; or when concerned about a sibling being victimized. A direct disclosure could be an out-of-the-blue statement prompted by a child's own fear, anguish, or frustration over the victimization. A disclosure might even be made as you share with your child the safety conversations covered in this book.

No matter how a disclosure comes out, you will best help your child by doing the following things:

1. Remain calm. Do not overreact.

Children who consider telling a parent about being touched in a "not okay" way might be facing some daunting thoughts: *How will my parent react? Will my parent believe me? Will I be in trouble? Will [the abuser] hurt me for telling? Will [the abuser] go to jail?*

When your child discloses, you will not immediately know what grooming tactics the offender has employed. It is therefore very important that you do not overreact to what has been shared because the reaction might feed into the fears the offender has planted in your child's mind.

Responses To Avoid

- "Oh, you must have misunderstood. He loves you."
- "He would never hurt you."
- "How could you say that about him?"
- "Are you telling the truth?"
- "I'm going to kill him!"
- "He's going to jail!"
- "How could you let that happen?"
- "Why didn't you tell me sooner?"
- "Why didn't you stop it?"

Unchecked, the pendulum can swing from denial, to chastisement, to accusations, to all-out revenge. None of these responses is helpful to a child who is crying out for help and support. Your child is mustering all the strength he or she has to tell what has happened—to let the secret out. The best response you can have is to be calm.

You could be in shock, horrified at what you just heard, worried for your child, and angry with the offender … but hold it together! Your child needs to see, and hear, a confident parent—one who listens, believes, and assures him that things are going to get better now that you know. Speak slowly and softly. (There will be a time and place where you can cry, scream, and vent with another adult—outside of your child's presence—but right now, your child needs you!)

To discover that someone has harmed the child you love will wound you deeply. But please understand that crying uncontrollably, or breathing angry threats of retaliation, only frightens your child more. Such strong reactions can cause your child to say nothing further—or even to recant.

2. Provide a safe place for your child to talk.

If the offender is present in the home or area, move your child to a separate location that is quiet, comfortable, and away from that person's presence. Give your child your complete attention.

3. Limit your questions. Do not ask for a lot of details.

Ask only the questions below (if your child has not already given the information.) Listen to the child's answers without interrupting. Let your child use his or her own words.

- What happened?
- When did it happen?
- Where did it happen?
- Who did it? (If you don't recognize the name, ask how your child knows the person.)

Later, write down what your child told you, putting his or her words in quotations. This will be helpful when reporting the matter to authorities.

4. Let your child know he or she is doing the right thing by telling you.

Affirm to your child that he or she is not at fault for what happened and has done nothing wrong. Assure your child that you believe him or her and that telling you was the right thing to do.

5. Don't promise to keep the matter a secret.

Let your child know that there are special people who help keep kids safe, and it is important for them to know what happened. If your child has a close relationship with the offender, you might say, "_____ *[offender's name] will need some help to stop doing that. These people can help you and help* _____ *[offender's name], too.*"

6. Report the matter immediately to your local law enforcement or Child Protective Services (CPS) agency.

Do not let your child talk with, or interact with, the offender for any reason. Law enforcement or CPS will be able to arrange for a professionally trained forensic interviewer to speak with your child to better determine what has happened. If a criminal act has been committed, law enforcement will talk with you about the next steps to be taken. Please do not think that family members or church elders are the proper persons to resolve a matter involving a sexual assault on a child. They are not!

7. Do not take matters into your own hands by confronting an offender.

This will tip off the offender that his secret is out. Doing so could greatly hinder the investigation and criminal case ahead. A parent who confronts a molester about sexually touching a child will likely hear an immediate denial or a minimization/explanation of his actions to vindicate himself. He might appear very concerned that his "innocent" actions were "mistaken" by your child. As a sign of "genuine" care, he might promise to "never make that mistake again" and to be extra aware of your child's sensitivities in the future. The offender might even suggest that your child has been abused, but by someone else. Resist the urge to confront. Remember there could be additional victims. *Contact the authorities and let them do their job.*

I remember bringing a man into headquarters one night to discuss the condition of his three-month-old daughter. We had come from Children's Hospital where the baby was in intensive care in critical condition. I believed this man had violently shaken his infant daughter, causing irreversible brain damage. As I walked him to the interview room we passed a detective who had a baby of the same age. This detective was a mountain of a man, his face was red, and his teeth were clenched. After seating the suspect in the interview room, I stepped out for a moment. The detective met me with an understandable comment, "Just give me five minutes with that guy, Diane." I reached up and gently patted his arm. "We'll get more from him doing it my way," I said.

Anyone with a heart could understand the anger that detective felt as a father. But displaying an angry, disgusted, or vengeful demeanor to this man was not going to help the situation. What I needed was for the suspect to talk to me. Getting a confession meant he had to see me as approachable, non-threatening, and trustworthy of knowing his secret. Maintaining my composure would keep the communication flowing.

It ended up being a challenging interview. The father was very guarded but did make statements that helped me build a case. By the end of my investigation he admitted everything and was sentenced to 18 years in prison.

Doing what is right by our children requires our time, effort, and selfless dedication. What could be more important or worthwhile? Over the years many people have asked me, "How do you deal with these kinds of crimes? You have to see and hear such horrible things. How can you stand these criminals?" The easiest answer is this: I am willing to do whatever is needed to ensure the protection of child victims and achieve justice for them. To stop a child molester means a child can start to heal, and many other children will be protected.

Nothing in my career has meant more.

Personal Notes

13

An Unexpected Future

This book began with the true case of four children whose lives were changed when the eldest, 11-year-old Cindy, disclosed years of sexual abuse by her stepfather. This case made an indelible mark on my life also; and ultimately brought me to tears when the verdict was read.

After interviewing Cindy I arranged for her to be examined by a trusted pediatrician, Dr. Marsh, who was a specially trained expert in child sexual assault matters. During the examination Dr. Marsha documented all of Cindy's statements about her sexual abuse. Everything was consistent with Cindy's interview with me. The physical examination showed Cindy had deep vaginal tears and virtually no hymen.

I asked Cindy's mom, Karen, to come in for an interview (remember, she had a third child abuse charge pending against her for physical abuse against Cindy). Karen arrived on time, very energetic, and all smiles. Karen knew her husband had obtained an attorney and that he was undecided about speaking with me and taking a polygraph exam. She told me that it was important to her to know what, if anything, had happened with Cindy. Karen had told her husband he needed to cooperate with the investigation and take the polygraph (which he never did).

Karen did not know I had interviewed Cindy already. I did not tell her, in order to see what answers she would give me if she felt I was uninformed.

I asked Karen to describe Cindy. Karen used words like "very sweet" and "very generous," but also said Cindy "can be very selfish" and was "flamboyant." The contradictions did not go unnoticed by me. When asked to describe her relationship with Cindy, Karen replied, "I have gotten from her teachers that she does a lot of things for attention." Karen then described Cindy as being "abusive" towards her younger brother. Karen described how the two siblings would frequently argue. Then, in almost an exhausted voice, she said, "I've gone through a lot of episodes with her."

Karen told of a time when Cindy took something from a classmate then lied to the teacher, claiming her mother gave her money to buy it. Karen told me that Cindy expected her to lie for Cindy in the matter, and added, "It's in my character to be honest. I could never do something like that." According to Karen, Cindy had a history of saying things about people that were not true.

Karen went on to say that she and Cindy were "very close," and "we talk all the time." Karen was sure Cindy would have confided in her if something bad had happened with the stepfather. Karen went to great lengths to tell me that she and her husband were wonderful, involved parents. One or both of them would go to teacher-parent meetings. She said Cindy was "very, very smart" and the *only* times Cindy's grades fell to Ds and Fs were the three times Cindy was in foster care.

Oh, yes ... foster care.

Karen didn't skip a beat in trashing her children's foster parents. "This last time weird things have been happening to all of them." Karen said the littlest, Mariah, had a bruise on her bottom when Mariah came to stay for a Christmas visit. Karen insisted she and her husband wanted to get Cindy into counseling "right away" because of this allegation of sexual abuse. They were concerned that some other foster child might be influencing Cindy to make a false accusation.

Karen brought up a situation somewhat out of the blue. She told how Cindy was playing with her cousins once when the family lived in Indiana. "They were putting pencils inside each other's vaginas!" Karen said with some alarm. She and her husband were quite upset and talked to family members about the incident. I asked, "You must have been terribly worried about her. Did you take her to the doctor to get her checked?" Karen said she immediately took Cindy to the hospital. Karen said the doctor checked her anally and vaginally. I asked about the results of the exam. "She was fine. Absolutely fine," said Karen. I asked for the name of the doctor and hospital. Karen couldn't remember, but said she had the information at home and would get it for me. I found her inability to remember the hospital's name rather telling.

I believe Karen was discrediting Cindy's character in hope that it would sway me from believing Cindy, and would lead to an end of the investigation. Karen portrayed herself as the doting mom who was protective of her children. But nothing could be further from the truth. There were a few things I learned about Karen that day. One, she was more devoted to her husband than to her children. Two, she was a liar. Three, she was narcissistic. Karen left the interview assuring me that Cindy would get counseling, and that she would tell her husband to take a polygraph to clear things up. I left the interview having obtained several statements I needed to investigate and verify.

I interviewed Cindy's teachers who remembered her as the sweet girl they were concerned for due to her introversion, grades, small size, and the bruises she would explain away. I obtained school records that showed the only times Cindy's grades made a significant improvement were *while* she was in foster care. I had copies of letters repeatedly sent by school officials to Cindy's parents asking for a meeting with them to discuss their concerns; letters that both parents had ignored.

I photographed three residences in Colorado where the family had resided. From my interview with Cindy I could see that her recollection of each location was accurate. I obtained multiple out-of-state police and Social Services' reports to gain insight to this family's history. I spoke with family members in Indiana who knew nothing of any pencil incident; nor did Cindy when I asked her. Karen never provided me the name of the hospital nor doctor who supposedly examined Cindy. The stepfather refused to talk with me and never took a polygraph.

I was certain Karen cunningly made up the story of the "pencils" to explain away any possible medical findings by Dr. Marsha. And despite her vow to get Cindy into counseling, Karen repeatedly refused to sign papers to allow Cindy to receive counseling while the investigation was ongoing. Odd as it might seem, Karen still had parental rights while the children were in foster care. In fact, anything Cindy requested Karen would not permit; things like getting a haircut, going to church with her foster family, or talking with a counselor. This was Karen and her husband's way of putting pressure on Cindy to recant the sexual abuse allegations. It was clear to me that Karen would do anything to protect her husband, even if he were a child molester.

How could a mother do that? How could anyone do that? Yet people do.

Sadly, sometimes tragically, people will believe adults over children.

Convincing a jury of this stepfather's guilt would be a challenge. People can't wrap their heads around the idea that someone who looks like them, holds down a job, acts politely, goes to church, and says all the right things … can be capable of such horrific acts. Most jurors do not understand the dynamics of child molestation. Cindy's molestation happened in secret. There were no eyewitnesses, no DNA, no video or photographs of the crime, no fingerprints, and no confession.

At trial, I testified to my interviews with Cindy, Karen, and other witnesses. I introduced into evidence the interview videotapes, drawings by Cindy, letters, and photographs. Others introduced medical, school, and Social Services records. Teri Camden testified to Cindy's initial outcry. I sat at the Prosecution's table as the Advisory Witness throughout the trial.

Dr. Marsha took the stand testifying about the vaginal damage she found in Cindy. The prosecutor asked if a pencil could cause the injuries. "Absolutely not," replied the doctor.

The key witness was Cindy herself. You could hear a pin drop when Cindy walked into the courtroom to testify at the trial. Tiny and soft-spoken, she carried a small afghan over one arm to provide her some comfort as she sat on the stand. Over the next several hours she described how the man who should have been her protector became her abuser.

Cindy said it started when "he got all mushy." He gave her hugs and kisses that were uncomfortable. Then the sexual touching began. Cindy testified she didn't like what was happening, but did not know what to do. He said he loved her and that she was special. She did like the gifts he gave her. Sometimes he promised to never do it again, but he always broke his promise. If she reminded him, he'd become angry and say, "Just do it!" Cindy said her stepfather told her this was their secret, and to never tell anyone or he could go to jail. The idea of him being away from home was frightening to Cindy since he was the only one who could intervene when her mom would beat her. So Cindy kept the secret for a long time.

This tiny little girl in this large, intimidating courtroom calmly answered every question posed to her. She described in detail the sexual acts that took place in multiple residences over the years. Never once did she waver from her original statement to me. The defense cross-examined her at length, even asking her to demonstrate a sexual position she described. (Some defense lawyers have no shame.)

The defense decided to make Karen the scapegoat, and she was willing to play the part. The defense focused on Karen's physical abuse of Cindy. They emphasized how Cindy loved her stepfather and relied on him to protect her from her mother. The defense argued that Cindy was lying about her stepfather in order to get away from Karen, permanently.

When Karen took the stand for the defense she described Cindy as being overly dramatic and untruthful. Karen admitted to not always being the best mom. She admitted punching and kicking Cindy, resulting in three foster placements for her children. Karen stated Cindy was only lying about the sexual abuse to get back at her. Karen, who testified two days after Dr. Marsha, even stood by her ridiculous story of how Cindy's cousins had penetrated Cindy vaginally, but not with a pencil as she told me in her interview. Now her testimony was that it was a marker!

The stepfather also took the stand. He testified how Karen beat Cindy unmercifully and how he pulled Karen off Cindy to try to protect her. He began to weep uncontrollably on the stand when describing the fury of Karen's anger, and the extent of cruelty Cindy endured. The judge allowed a break so he could regain his composure. When testimony resumed he talked of his love for Cindy and how he did not blame her for wanting to get back at her mother by accusing him. He adamantly denied *ever* touching her sexually.

The jury had to decide whom to believe. There were eight felony charges against Cindy's stepfather, and each carried a heavy prison sentence. The jury was out for two days deliberating. When we assembled in court to hear their verdict, I took the District Attorney's hand and whispered, *"If they find him guilty on the first count, they will find him guilty on all counts."* But I knew the reverse was true, too: if they found him "not guilty" on one, they would find him "not guilty" on all. Cindy's foster mother, Teri Camden, sat behind me in the gallery. We both knew that if he was found "not guilty"—Cindy and all her siblings would be going back to live in an unimaginable hell of a home.

The judge began to read: *"On count one, Sexual Assault on a Child by One in a Position of Trust, the jury finds the defendant ... guilty."* I cannot adequately describe the immense relief I felt at that moment. I put my head in my hands and began to cry. Imagine, the professional detective who never cries had tears running down her face. It was like the weight of the world had come off my shoulders. I never even heard the next seven verdicts. They were all "guilty." Never would that monster touch this child again.

I turned to look at Teri Camden. We smiled, nodded, and wiped our tears. It was this woman's unconditional love for her foster child that opened the door for Cindy to finally trust someone and tell her long-held secret.

I never doubted the sincerity of this child victim.

Children are not capable of spinning or maintaining complex lies. They cannot have intimate knowledge of sexual acts based simply on their own imaginations. Such knowledge comes from experience. Children can be intimidated, manipulated, and bullied into silence for years because they feel they have no one to turn to, or that no one would believe them.

Fortunately, the jury understood this.

In his evaluation prior to sentencing—and I believe in an attempt to garner a lighter sentence—the stepfather admitted to having sexual contact with Cindy. But he refused to admit to committing the more egregious acts. At sentencing the judge chastised him for his perjury on the stand and for unnecessarily dragging Cindy through an arduous trial process. The judge stated this was the worst case of child sexual abuse ever tried in his courtroom. The stepfather was sentenced to 32 years-to-life in prison.

In the months that followed Karen lost all parental rights to her four children.

And Cindy? She was adopted by a loving family … the Camdens.

As the years went by I kept in touch with Cindy and her adoptive mom, Teri. Cindy received a few years of excellent counseling from a therapist who specializes in child sexual abuse victims. Teen years held special challenges as Teri taught Cindy about proper boundaries for dating. One June I received a graduation announcement with Cindy's senior picture. She looked beautiful! Next came a job she enjoyed, and then, a special guy. Cindy married a wonderful young man who understood her past and loved her all the more. I was thrilled the day I held their first-born baby.

Healing is never fast, but healing does happen. There can be an unexpected and hopeful future for abused children who receive the patient, nurturing love they deserve.

My hope is that you create a bond of trust with your child that no molester can easily break. Applying the steps in this book will empower you to have honest, age-appropriate conversations with your children about their bodies; and to instill in them an understanding that their bodies deserve respect. The time you take to lovingly converse with and instruct your child will give your child the *confidence to come talk with you* should anyone threaten his or her innocence.

* * *

There are many things in life worth doing, many admirable goals we can strive to achieve. But, to me, nothing is more important than investing in the lives of children. My thirty years in law enforcement have given me countless opportunities to intervene in crisis situations where children needed protection. I am humbled to have had such a privilege.

Being a parent was your destiny. My heart's desire is that you treasure the little ones entrusted to your care by making their well-being your top priority in life. I encourage you to make meaningful two-way conversations a daily activity with your child. Be your child's confidant. Become the person to whom *everything* is an open book. Intentionally earn that special trust. Your nurturing love, caring instruction, and wise protective choices will help your child enjoy a safe, fun, and innocent childhood.

It has been my joy to contribute to that end through what I have shared in this book.

Life takes all kinds of turns. When I was young, becoming a mother was my heart's desire. It never happened. But now, when people ask me about my children, I smile. I tell them, "God has given me many children, just not in the way I expected."

Being a detective in the field of crimes against children has been my most treasured work. It was my destiny. And I wouldn't have had it any other way.

Personal Notes

Acknowledgments

I started writing *Protecting Innocence* to share with parents the insights I gained from over a decade of investigating crimes against children. My career has been one of responding to crimes; but now I wanted to prevent them. I am grateful to others who came along side me to help bring *Protecting Innocence* to its completion. Some contributed creative talents, others gave critical feedback, and many prayed. All shared the desire to see children protected.

I want to thank my friend, editor, and head cheerleader, Rick Marschall. His keen literary eye and patient listening ear assisted me immeasurably. His editorial skills and his creative illustrations helped communicate this book's message.

The talented Nick Zelinger of NZ Graphics did a wonderful job designing the book's cover and interior layout.

I met Dr. Kathryn Wells in an emergency room where she was treating an infant with seventeen fractures. While she saved the child's life, I got a confession from the perpetrator. Dr. Wells is an amazing pediatrician and child abuse expert. I was honored that she wrote the Foreword to *Protecting Innocence*.

Many persons read my manuscript to help insure the book's objectives were on target and clearly communicated. Their feedback was very valuable. Among these readers were moms, dads, grandparents, teachers, therapists, medical professionals, attorneys, law enforcement, and social workers. I was blessed that each enthusiastically affirmed the need for this book.

My heartfelt thanks to Denise Aulie, Chief Phil Baca (Ret), Dana Jene Easter, J.D., Robin Eskey, Psy.D, Nancy Kay, LPC, Christina Klumph, Cheryl Meakins, Cecil Murphey, Peggy Rupple, Dr. Bob Summers, Steve and Deb Woodworth. My appreciation to the late Mary Taft for her sweet friendship and encouragement. Special thanks to Sue Summers and Penny Carlavato for fanning the creative fires. And thanks to Verna Pauls for saying years ago, "Diane, you need to write a book!"

Thanks to the Jefferson County Sheriff's Office in Colorado for its commitment to excellence and service to the community. I am proud to be "a green shirt." Thanks to my longtime Crimes Against Children partner, Detective Lee Hoag—we made a great team!

My humble thanks to God who called me to this profession and gave me the privilege of being an extension of His comfort—and an instrument of His justice—in a fallen world.

Thanks to all my wonderful family, especially Mom, Denise, Peggy, Tom and Mike. Laughing with you is the best! You make life more joyful and every burden lighter. I love you all so very much.

Contact Detective Diane

Website: www.ProtectingInnocence.com
Facebook: Protecting Innocence Book
Schedule book signings:
DetectiveDiane@gmail.com

Have Detective Diane speak to your organization:

- Parenting organizations
- Women's groups
- Educators
- Social Workers
- Law Enforcement
- Civic organizations
- Faith-based organizations

E-mail: DetectiveDiane@gmail.com
to schedule a presentation.

Anatomical Drawings

The following pages contain anatomically correct drawings of a young male and female child. The drawings can be helpful in teaching your child the appropriate names of private body parts. Please refer back to Chapter 4 (*The Proper Names for Intimate Parts*) for assistance in understanding how this discussion can take place. *Remember: these drawings are **not** to be used to question a child about suspected sexual abuse.*

Male Anatomical Drawing

Male Anatomical Drawing

Female Anatomical Drawing

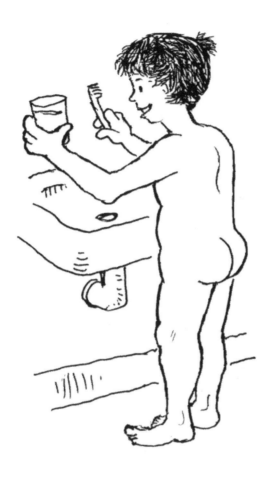

Female Anatomical Drawing

Resources For Parents And Caregivers

APSAC – American Professional Society on the Abuse
of Children's Advocacy Center
877.40A.PSAC
http://apsac.fmhi.usf.edu/index.asp

National Children's Advocacy Center
256.533.0531
www.nationalcac.org

National Center for Missing and Exploited Children
703.274.3900
www.missingkids.com

Office of Juvenile Justice and Delinquency Prevention
(OJJDP)
800.851.3420
http://ojjdp.ncjrs.org/

Prevent Child Abuse America
312.663.3520
www.preventchildabuse.org

Native American Children's Alliance
216.321.7989
www.nativechildalliance.org
choctawcaf@yahoo.com

American Prosecutors Research Institute National District
Attorneys Association
703-549-9222
www.ndaa.org

Child Welfare League of America
202.638.2952
www.cwla.org

FAITH-BASED RESOURCES FOR MALE SURVIVORS
OF CHILD SEXUAL ABUSE:

Website: Shattering the Silence—Cecil Murphey,
menshatteringthesilence.blogspot.com
Book: *When The Man You Loved Was Abused* –
Cecil Murphey; Kregel Publications

About The Author

Diane Obbema, a 30-year veteran of the Jefferson County Sheriff's Office in Colorado, specialized for 12 years as a detective investigating crimes against children in Colorado's First Judicial District.

The first woman ever to be named Top Recruit in a Jefferson County Law Enforcement Academy, Deputy Diane worked several years on patrol before being selected to pioneer the DARE program in the Jefferson County Schools in 1990. After returning to patrol, she was promoted to Detective in 1998 and assigned to the Crimes Against Children Unit. Over the years Detective Diane investigated hundreds of child abuse cases resulting in convictions of perpetrators. She has served as a Crime Scene Technician, Field Training Instructor, and a P.O.S.T. Certified Law Enforcement Academy Instructor.

An accomplished speaker and presenter, Detective Diane has instructed university students, child welfare professionals, and law enforcement officers throughout Colorado on topics such as: The Mind of a Child Molester; Child Forensic Interviewing; and Interview and Interrogation of Child Molesters.

Detective Diane was honored as the 2006 Employee of the Year for her excellence in directing the department's Sex Offender Registry. Detective Diane's interrogation skills were used in obtaining confessions from suspects in the nation's first multi-jurisdictional Internet Predator Sting. Her testimony before Colorado's Senate and House of Representatives resulted in stronger sex offender legislation.

Detective Diane earned wide recognition for her notable work in several high-profile crimes. She was a key investigator of the Columbine High School shootings, earning commendations for her work to determine exact events in the school library where 10 children were murdered and many others severely injured or traumatized.

Her central role in the Evergreen "Rebirthing" Homicide case—where a child was killed by her therapists—received national and international coverage. The case prompted new legislation protecting children from the use of physical restraints during any similar "therapeutic" technique.

Three times Detective Diane has received commendations by the Jefferson County District Attorney's Office for her investigations of child abuse cases. She received the

Hero's Award given by the Jefferson County Children's Advocacy Center. Detective Diane served as Chair and 10-year member of the Jefferson County Child Protection Team.

Detective Diane has received her agency's Professional Conduct Award, Sheriff's Commendation, Life Saving Award, and the prestigious Sheriff's Distinguish Service Medal. Over her career she received letters of commendation from schools, civic organizations, citizens, and other law enforcement agencies. Detective Diane has volunteered as an Investigative Associate with International Justice Missions, a human rights agency that intervenes on behalf of child victims of the sex trafficking industry.

Detective Diane became a recruiter and background investigator for her agency's Professional Standards Division in 2009, while continuing to instruct in law enforcement academies on Crimes Against Children. She retires in 2015 to devote herself to speaking on child abuse investigation and prevention.

www.ProtectingInnocence.com

Made in the USA
San Bernardino, CA
02 March 2015